D0626651

Knowledge is Light

Previous volumes published from ASTENE conferences:

Desert Travellers from Herodotus to T E Lawrence (2000) edited by Janet Starkey and Okasha El Daly. Durham, ASTENE.

Travellers in the Levant: Voyagers and Visionaries (2001) edited by Sarah Searight and Malcolm Wagstaff. Durham, ASTENE.

Egypt Through the Eyes of Travellers (2002) edited by Paul Starkey and Nadia El Kholy. Durham, ASTENE.

Travellers in the Near East (2004) edited by Charles Foster. London, Stacey International.

Women Travellers in the Near East (2005) edited by Sarah Searight. ASTENE and Oxbow Books.

Who Travels Sees More (2007) edited by Diane Fortenberry. Oxford, ASTENE and Oxbow Books.

Saddling the Dogs (2009) edited by Diane Fortenberry and Deborah Manley. Oxford, ASTENE and Oxbow Books.

Knowledge is Light

Travellers in the Near East

ASTENE
and
Oxbow Books
Oxford and Oakville

Published by
Oxbow Books, Oxford, UK

© Oxbow Books and the individual authors, 2011

ISBN 978-1-84217-448-7

A CIP record for this book is available from the British Library

This book is available direct from:

Oxbow Books, Oxford, UK
(Phone: 01865-241249; Fax: 01865-794449)

and

The David Brown Book Company
PO Box 511, Oakville, CT 06779, USA
(Phone: 860-945-9329; Fax: 860-945-9468)

or from our website
www.oxbowbooks.com

Library of Congress Cataloging-in-Publication Data

Knowledge is light : travellers in the Near East / edited by Katherine Salahi.
    p. cm.
Includes bibliographical references and index.
ISBN 978-1-84217-448-7
    1. Travellers--Middle East--Biography. 2. Explorers--Middle East--Biography. 3. Middle East--Discovery and exploration. 4. Middle East--Description and travel. I. Salahi, Katherine.
G225.K57 2011
915.604'150922--dc23
                    2011023276

Cover photograph © J. Perdios Collection, Greece

Printed and bound in Great Britain by
Information Press, Eynsham, Oxfordshire

Contents

Introduction

For thousands of years travellers wandered to, and spread out through, Egypt and the Near East, seeking trade, adventure and knowledge. The amethysts set in the fifth-century gold jewellery of Britain's great Staffordshire Hoard (discovered early this century) can be traced back to Afghanistan, and must have been carried by travellers through the region, following the Silk Road into Europe and eventually onward into England. For centuries travellers to – and from – the Near East carried knowledge with them and then carried home the new knowledge acquired in the region. And knowledge, as the Arabic proverb states, is light.

These links have always continued. The Association for the Study of Travel in Egypt and the Near East (ASTENE) was set up in 1997 to follow, study and record the experience of travel and travellers in the region. The accounts in this collection of papers are chosen from the wide-ranging programme offered at the ASTENE conference held in the summer of 2009 at Durham University, as being linked by a search for knowledge by travellers to the region, and by their use of their own knowledge within the region. This spectrum of time and place has been brought together in date order of the journeys. The resulting book, published at the Association's conference in Oxford in 2011, joins the books which have arisen from earlier conferences – both in Britain and in the ASTENE region during study visits there.

The travels which are the subjects of these papers are widely spread through space and through time. Lucy Pollard writes of John Covel, who was at Constantinople in the 1670s at a time when the European commercial links with the Ottoman Empire had brought the two regions into closer contact, and knowledge of each other was increasingly spread. John Covel brought a huge store of learning with him, especially from the classical world, when he became Chaplain in Constantinople, and took away, in his voluminous but little-known diaries, an extraordinary account of what it was like to be an Englishman in late seventeenth-century Greece and Asia Minor. The Levant traders who John Covel and others served grew the trade between Europe and the world and the Levant. By establishing trade routes, they made it easier for others to follow and become more involved in the life of the Near East and beyond.

Some travellers' accounts were less than sympathetic towards Islam, in interpretations that depicted the Islamic world at that period. By contrast James Rennell, in the early- to mid-nineteenth century, was a scientific observer of the area and of past travellers' interpretations of it.

The Reverend Robert Master (1794–1867), who accompanied Sir Archibald Edmonstone to Egypt in 1819, set out from the Nile to explore the oases of the Western desert and then journeyed onward through the Holy Land in 1820, and home through Greece. Master took his biblical knowledge of the region within him, and returned with accounts of contemporary life. Willey Reveley, an architect and artist, was employed by an English 'milord', and gave the world important interpretations of ancient Greek architecture.

Later, in the early 1860s, the French philosopher Ernest Renan, while on an archaeological expedition in the Near East, wrote a biography of Jesus, set in the true reality of the landscapes in which Jesus wandered, thus offering a Jesus who was 'alive', whom Renan 'had met under the blue heaven of Galilee'.

Another quarter of a century later, the Constantinople-born Greek, Theodore Ralli (1852–1909), an orientalist-genre painter who spent months each year in Cairo, in 1885 turned to Athos to seek out where 'the most pure tradition of Byzantine art was preserved'. Maria-Mirka Palioura shows how his experience of travel to Athos, and the new knowledge he gained, changed his art. John Chapman uses the example of clothing to discuss how travellers – although they took in the knowledge of local customs – still remained between the two worlds of East and West.

Often the travellers illustrated their accounts, providing views of places previously known only by their names, like the seventeenth-century drawings of the Topkapi Palace and Aya Sophia in Constantinople. Such early accounts describe Muslim life as well as buildings – although that life was seen and reported on by men with 'a deeply embedded Christian polemical tradition regarding Islam', and travellers often reviled the unfamiliar life they saw, returning home with 'knowledge' which was not always 'light'. Some accounts even equated the origins of Islam with the devil; others were equally offensive – to modern readers – about Jews and Judaism, in the common currency of the times. It would be good to be able to say that such attitudes are no longer acceptable today.

Travellers' tales and interpretations were passed with little change from one traveller to another, and eager listeners and readers back home happily absorbed the prejudices of travellers along with their knowledge. William Lithgow in 1616 even decried 'the Turks' for having 'no bels in the Churches'. Prejudice, particularly about the otherwise unknown, is easily absorbed, and false knowledge can pass from mouth to mouth, making 'knowledge' sometimes nearer darkness than light.

Anders Ingram points out in his 'Depictions of Islam' that the churchman Thomas Smith (1671) approached Islam 'already certain of the truth and validity of the venerable Christian polemical tradition regarding it, and saw no reason or need to delve deeper or engage with its ideas'. Few such travellers, Ingram concludes, 'were led to question what they already "knew" from this tradition'.

The two papers by Peta Rée and Patricia Usick, both founder members of ASTENE, take the accounts of two travellers in the late eighteenth century, who met in Rome and travelled together: Sir Richard Worsley and 'his artist', Willey Reveley. In the time before photography, rich travellers who could not draw were wont to engage an artist, often met on their journey. Sir Richard's written descriptions, however, were lively and factual and created pictures of Greece, Egypt and Turkey – and the common women of Mykonos – in the mind. He swept through Egypt and around its sights, both real and legendary, bringing both knowledge and ignorance to all he saw, including the famed departure of the Mecca Caravan from Cairo. In Constantinople he wrote one of the most detailed descriptions of the encounter between the Grand Signior and the foreigner, fearfully interpreted by a terrified Greek Dragoman. Welcomed to Constantinople by the English Ambassador, Sir Robert Ainslie, Sir Richard had good opportunities to see and visit many of the great sites. But, despite the title of Peta Rée's paper, he was *not* captured by pirates.

Patricia Usick's paper provides the 'other side of the coin': the architect/artist Willey Reveley's account of his journeying with Sir Richard Worsley. Both men kept copious journals, making their travels among the best documented of the period, especially as Reveley's topographical drawings are all titled and dated, and his diary – rather more concerned with antiquity than his employer's – provides a very readable account of sites at this time. The accounts in her paper come from his unpublished diaries.

In Constantinople, after travelling together for months, the two men parted company, with some animosity. Reveley carried on to Russia and encountered the social reformer, Jeremy Bentham, who, intriguingly, had spent two months in Constantinople. Returning to Rome, Reveley met and married Maria James, a fascinating young woman only mentioned here in passing, who returned with him to London. Reveley's published records of the antiquities of Greece gave him a lasting place in accounts and records of travel. The tale of the loss and recovery of the drawings owned by Worsley makes dramatic reading. Reveley was a traveller who deserves to be better known and more widely read, who gave to the world a much clearer understanding and knowledge of the architecture of ancient Greece than they had previously enjoyed.

The traveller of the next paper, by Janet Starkey (another founder member of ASTENE), is James Rennell (1742–1830), who, after a long military career in India, had acquired great expertise in surveying and hydrography. He retired from India through ill health and spent the next thirty years researching at East India House in London, becoming recognised, by 1825, as 'one of the first geographers of this or any other age'. He studied both classical and modern sources, including the 'Oriental geographers' – the Arab authorities like al-Idris (1100–62) and Ibn Hawqal (943–88). Rennell's work provided useful knowledge to travellers who followed after him. Splendidly intriguing was his study of the rate of travel by camels to establish distances. He was, with other travellers in Egypt and the Near East, a member of the African Association, which would later be absorbed into the Royal Geographical Society.

Deborah Manley

Acknowledgements

ASTENE thanks the authors of each of the essays included in this, our seventh book, for sharing the fruits of their researches and for working to bring their papers together for publication. Through this coming together of such varied research more is added to our knowledge of the Near East through time – and that knowledge is light ...

The Authors

John Chapman is a Principal Lecturer at the University of Hertfordshire. His passion is the history of the Mani Peninsula, Greece, publishing a number of academic papers as well as the acclaimed website http://www.maniguide.info. He is currently researching the 1839 Greek travel diaries of the 3rd Earl of Carnarvon.

Anders Ingram, since completing his PhD at Durham University in 2010, has published a number of articles and taught at Durham University. His research interests include early modern English writing on the Ottoman Turks and Islam, travel writing, historical and geographical literature, and the history of the book.

Deborah Manley, a founder member of ASTENE, worked in educational publishing for Europe and Africa. She and her sister Peta Rée wrote a biography of the British Consul General in Egypt 1818–27 (Libri). She has also published a number of anthologies about travellers in Egypt with another ASTENE member, Dr Sahar Abdel Hakim.

Geoffrey Nash, PhD, is Senior Lecturer in English at Sunderland University. His research specialisms include Orientalism and nineteenth-century Orientalists, and Middle East travel writing. Recent publications include *From Empire to Orient: Travellers to the Middle East, 1830–1926* (I.B.Tauris 2005) and *Travellers to the Middle East from Burkhardt to Thesiger: An Anthology* (Anthem 2009).

Maria-Mirka Palioura studied French Letters and Art History (BA, PhD Athens University, MA Université Paris I Panthèon-Sorbonne). She has edited two books and presented several conference papers on nineteenth-century Greek art, has worked in the Greek Ministry of Culture, and is a Member of the Hellenic Association of Art Historians.

Lucy Pollard, after taking a classics degree, had a career as a librarian, book indexer and teacher. In retirement, she did a PhD at Birkbeck College London on Britons in Greece and Asia Minor in the seventeenth century. She has travelled widely in Greece and the Middle East.

Peta Rée, having enjoyed her first voyage, from India to England, at the age of 16 months, has been travelling intermittently ever since. In between, she has read many travellers' tales and even contributed to the genre, including co-authoring *Henry Salt* with Deborah Manley.

Janet Starkey, MA, MPhil, lectures in Archaeology at Durham University. She has lived with nomads in Jordan and Sudan, and has worked in Jordan, Oman, Qatar, Kuwait and Egypt. She has published several books about travellers in the Middle East, and is Editor-in-Chief of the Proceedings of the Seminar for Arabian Studies.

Patricia Usick studied Egyptology at University College London. Her PhD thesis was on the Egyptian and Nubian drawings and journal of William John Bankes (1786–1855). She is Honorary Archivist in the Department of Egypt and the Sudan, the British Museum, where she researches the history of the collection.

John Covel: a Levant Company Chaplain at Constantinople in the 1670s

Lucy Pollard

Figure 1. Portrait of John Covel by Valentine Ritz. By kind permission of Christ's College, Cambridge.

On New Year's Day 1671 (n.s.), John Covel recorded in his diary 'I entred upon my employment.' He had arrived in Constantinople the previous day, on the *London Merchant* (Anderson 1989, 148), and his employment was his position as chaplain to the ambassador. The first thing he did was to collect his luggage from the customs officials, who to his horror 'ript open my Trunks and boxes, and searched and rifled everything' (BL MS Add. 22912: 74r). To his great relief, only one of the books he had brought was missing. Books were of crucial importance to Covel, who had spent his adult life to date at Christ's College, Cambridge, and who was already, at the age of 32, a man of considerable learning, speaking several ancient and modern languages and having a huge store of knowledge about the classics. His account of his experiences in Turkey, preserved in three volumes of diaries in the British Library (BL MSS Add. 22912, 22913, 22914), is deeply coloured by his classical background. References to and quotations from a wide range of classical authors appear throughout the text.

These voluminous diaries have on the whole been mentioned only in passing by modern scholars (with the honourable exception of J.-P. Grélois), yet they are an extraordinary treasure-chest of evidence for what it was like to be an Englishman in Greece and Asia Minor towards the end of the seventeenth century. Their value lies not least in the fact that although parts (such as a 'set-piece' description of court ceremonies in Adrianople) seem to have been intended for publication, much of the writing displays an immediacy and frankness that might well have been lost had they ever appeared in print. We not only learn about conditions of life in the expatriate community, and Covel's reactions to his encounters with people, places and events, but also get a vivid picture of his own personality. The space available here allows me just to touch on some of the topics of interest to the reader.

Constantinople at this period was a large cosmopolitan city, where Covel met Greeks, Jews, Albanians, Armenians and other Europeans as well as Turks. Its population was getting on for 600,000 (Cambridge, in contrast, had fewer than 8,000 inhabitants in the early eighteenth century). The gradual readmission of the Jews to England from the middle of the seventeenth century had given rise to small Jewish communities in London, but Covel is unlikely ever to have knowingly met a Jew before his arrival in the Levant. His reactions, though widely shared at the time, are nevertheless shocking to modern ears. When he went with the diplomatic entourage to take part in the ambassador's audience with the Sultan in Adrianople, he found himself lodged in a Jewish house. He writes (BL MS Add. 22912: 187v) that:

> The house we first were allotted, was the damnedest confounded place that ever mortall man was put into. It was a jewes house, not half big enough to hold half my Ld's family, a meer nest of fleas and cimici [bugs], and rats and mice, and stench surrounded with whole kennels of nasty beastly Jewes.

One end of the town has no decent houses,

> being all Jewes, crouded two or three families into a house that hath not more roomes. If the old Jewes were such poisonous beasts I must needs allow their frequent washings, and think they needed not touch a dead body to be unclean, for they could not touch a living one without being so.

And yet, on the eve of his departure from Constantinople he wrote a long letter to his Cambridge colleague Henry More, the neoplatonist, giving a sympathetic account of a heterodox Jewish sect (Christ's archives 21/28). Such ambivalence is common for the period, and may perhaps be put down to the fact that Judaism was seen in a different light from actual Jews, as Glaser has convincingly demonstrated (Glaser 2007).

Like many of his classically-educated contemporaries who visited Greece, Covel thought that the Greek people had sadly deteriorated from their glory days, and that the spoken Greek language was a travesty of ancient Greek. He found few Greeks with any degree of education: even priests and monks fell short of his expectations. Nevertheless, for the rest of his long life (he died at the age of 84 after a career spent mainly in Cambridge) he carried on a learned correspondence in Greek with Greek churchmen. As the first Englishman to visit Mount Athos, he provided information about the Holy Mountain which another Englishman, Paul Rycaut, incorporated into one of his widely-read works (Rycaut 1679, 216–63). He appreciated the hospitality offered by the monks. At Lavra, for example, Covel and his party were provided with mules saddled with carpets for the ride up from the shore, were received with great respect, and fed on fish, oil, houseleeks, beans, onions, garlic, olives, herbs, pepper, salt, saffron, and oranges, all washed down with good wine (BL MS Add. 22914: 44v).

Of course, Covel met Turks as well as Greeks, and here again his reactions are mixed. He admired the orderliness and quiet behaviour of the crowd at a court ceremony (BL MS Add. 22912: 195v):

> Amongst so many people it was most wonderfull to see the order and strange silence; not the least rudenesse in boyes or men... I never met the least affront..., but rather extraordinary kindnesse...[;] amongst these vast multitudes all are as hushed and orderly as we are at a sermon. I could not possibly beleive it till I found it alwayes so.

A few pages later, however (BL MS Add. 22912: 202v), he records that

> I should heartily have commended their piety, had I not seen in the very same place all the roguery and beastlinesse of buggery and the like acted there publickly with the applause and approbation of the cheif men amongst them as well as the rabble.

Sexual excess of various kinds was a common allegation made by Europeans against Turks, and Covel is not unusual here.

Covel was interested in all sorts of things: science and medicine, antiquities, plants, the Orthodox church, etymology, codes and food among other things. Curiously, the one aspect of his life about which we hear almost nothing is his work as a chaplain. On the morning of the departure of the ambassador and his party for Adrianople, he records that there were prayers and a sermon, and another Englishman, Francis Vernon, who met Covel in Constantinople, records (Royal Society MS 73: 59r) that he heard him give a sermon on the subject 'we shall have sorrow in this world', but we know almost nothing about how he went about his daily work. References to and quotations from the Bible in his diaries are far outnumbered by those from classical authors. He certainly seems to have had plenty of leisure time, much of which he used to travel to sites of historical interest near Constantinople or the Aegean coast. One trip he made, in company with other members of the diplomatic and commercial community, was to Bursa, the old Ottoman capital. During this journey, his friend and companion, Mr Cary, fell ill and was unable to continue the journey to Smyrna. Although there was a doctor in the party, it was Covel, described by another of the party as Cary's 'Spiritual Physician' (Wheler 1682, 223), who stayed behind with him. But the account in Covel's diary of what followed reads like a medical doctor's clinical notes on the case rather than the description of a priest or a friend. Cary died after 13 days and was buried in the Armenian cemetery (BL MS Add. 22912: 249v–250r).

Perhaps it was precisely because his official duties were not very onerous that he was able to do so much travelling during his years in the Levant. Apart from his trip to Adrianople for ambassador Sir John Finch's audience with the sultan, and a voyage which he made to accompany the body of his first ambassador from Constantinople to Smyrna (both of which were official), he made several journeys out of personal interest. In the autumn of 1675 he spent three weeks visiting the islands of the Sea of Marmara and the Asia Minor coast; the next year he was away for over two months, seeing Magnesia (near Ephesus) and Bursa among other places, and the following February he travelled to Iznik/Nicaea. When he left Constantinople for the final time, he went to Mount Athos.

One of Covel's main interests, and the reason for many of these journeys, was the ruins of classical and early Christian sites such as Ephesus. Although other travellers had visited such sites (and the supposed ruins of Troy, for example, were a particularly popular destination), the 1670s saw the beginnings of a new attitude to antiquities, a kind of proto-archaeology involving the attempt to understand the history and layout of buildings and towns. Covel's long description of Ephesus demonstrates this: here was an extremely confusing site, partly because the coastline had changed since ancient times, partly because the city had gone through many stages over time, and not least because the only available guidebooks were the *Geography* of Strabo and Pausanias' *Guide to Greece*, written 17 and 15 centuries before respectively. Covel made valiant attempts to sort out the topography and to record what he saw. He gives a long account of a piece of relief sculpture, which is in fact a Roman sarcophagus now in the Woburn Abbey collection (Angelicoussis 1992, 79), but at the time was built into a wall. It is to his credit that, in spite of mistaking the subject, he recognised that the slabs had been set in the wrong order (BL MS Add. 22912: 47r–51v).

One notable characteristic of Covel's comments about antiquities is the way in which he stresses the tentative nature of his conclusions: phrases like 'meer conjecture' and 'a meer maybe' crop up frequently. Like other contemporary travellers, Francis Vernon, George Wheler and Wheler's French companion Jacob Spon, he was constantly measuring, counting, and making sketches and diagrams. Sometimes he guessed dimensions by pacing them out, and the pages of his diaries are full of the inscriptions which he transcribed, though sometimes this was made difficult by the lack of a 'perspective glass' or telescope.

Interestingly, Covel only occasionally draws a distinction between pagan and Christian antiquities. The subject of attitudes to paganism and Christianity, and the way in which seventeenth century culture was rooted in both, is too large to embark on here, but it is worth remembering that Christ appears as Pan in both Spenser's *Shepherd's calendar* and Milton's *Hymn on the morning of Christ's nativity*.

Covel was constantly frustrated by the lack or inaccuracy of maps. From the island of Chalchis in the Sea of Marmara he tried to make a map of some of the other islands, but having no compass, he writes (BL MS Add. 22912: 249r) that he 'laid them down by my bare eye, yet I fancy they are very near the truth, unlesse being upon Chalchis caused me to make that biggest[,] it appearing so to my eye then'. In Adrianople, he obtained permission to go up to the top of the minaret of Sultan Selim's mosque, which helped him to verify the accuracy of a map he had made of the city (BL MS Add. 22912: 232r).

I said earlier that one of the interests of the diaries lies in the picture it gives us of Covel's personality. So what was he like? He was an extremely learned man, but one who did not wear his learning lightly, and rarely used one word when ten would do. He was conscious of his own status as a man of the cloth: on one occasion some friendly Armenian priests delighted him by calling him to join them at the communion rails of their church (BL MS Add. 22912: 253v), and conversely he was extremely annoyed to be excluded from the ambassador's audience with the sultan, especially since the ambassador himself had promised him he *would* be included (BL MS Add. 22912: 234v). But he could laugh at himself: part of his diary appears to have been a kind of extended letter to a friend at home in Cambridge, to whom at one point he describes the difficulty of correcting the errors of previous mapmakers. Presumably referring to the didactic nature of his description, he adds (BL MS Add. 22912: 188r) 'You se[e] how parsonlike I write to you.'

In Cyzicus he searched for a spring mentioned in Pliny (*Historia naturalis* 31.6) which was said to cure the pangs of love, and found two possible candidates (BL MS Add. 22914: 30r): 'I drank of both ... to see if I might find the cure mention'd in Pliny wrought upon myself; perhaps neither is it [i.e. the right one].' As a fellow of Christ's, he was required to be celibate, but he was certainly susceptible to feminine charms: he particularly appreciated the women of Chios (according to several travellers the most attractive in Greece), referring to one as having 'great lovely black eyes' (BL MS Add. 22914: 61r). He also has a line in scatological humour, being much amused, for example, by the little hillocks beside the road to Adrianople, which he was told (BL MS Add. 22912: 217r) marked the places where the Grand Seigneur had 'eased himself..., in plain english pist'.

His attention to detail was prodigious, and he was frequently irritated by having to hurry over ruins because his companions were in too much haste. On one page, the phrase 'the hurry we were in' is scribbled across the middle of a page of archaeological notes, without any context (BL MS Add. 22912: 270r). Although he sometimes comes across as a fussy man, he was obviously quite intrepid as a traveller. To see one Ephesus building properly he was forced to wriggle flat on his stomach, and on another journey he and his servant took a detour away from the main party, causing the rest some anxiety (BL MS Add. 22912: 242r): 'I could persuade no man to accompany me, fear of theives and a calf with a white face disheartened them all; away went my man and I.'

He was also deeply rooted in his home landscape of East Anglia, frequently comparing sights seen in the Levant to remembered scenes of home. Seeing buildings washed away by the sea he recalls Cromer in Norfolk, and a river is described as 'about the bignesse of Cam' (BL MS Add. 22912: 259r–v). In his account of a grand procession to celebrate a court ceremony he even uses an East Anglian dialect word, 'jibby-horse', that is, a dressed-up horse.

Covel was an urbane man and also a complicated one, and in spite of all we learn about him it is only rarely that we feel he is speaking straight from the heart, so when this does happen it is all the more striking. The day of his final departure from Constantinople, which happened to be his 39th birthday, was clearly a day of deep emotion (BL MS Add. 22914: 27r):

> This day in the year 1638 I was born at 2 a clock in the morning being Monday, and it pleased me to se[e] so many things meet this day, whereby I may reckon it my second birth... This day I left Stambol ... It pleased god I was wth more respect then I deserved treated by all at my parting, and finally accompanyed by my friends to the seaside wth a kind of painfull joy and brought as it was to a new life, just as my Mother in [throes?] and pangs, had a mixture of joy when a son was borne into the world.

Covel's desire to travel to exotic places seems to have been sated by his years in the Levant; notwithstanding a reference in his only published work, which appeared at the very end of his life, to the itinerant life he had led (Covel 1722, Preface), in fact he spent much of the remainder of his life in Cambridge. But on 23 November 1695, John Evelyn recorded in his diary that he had dined with 'the great oriental traveller', John Covel. It seems that Covel dined out on his experiences for many years.

BIBLIOGRAPHY

Manuscripts
British Library MS Add. 22912, Covel diary.
British Library MS Add. 22913, Covel diary.
British Library MS Add. 22914, Covel diary.
Christ's College, Cambridge, archives, box 21, item 28, Covel letter.
Royal Society MS 73, Vernon diary.

Publications
Anderson, S. (1989) *An English consul in Turkey: Paul Rycaut at Smyrna, 1667–1678.* Oxford, Clarendon Press.
Angelicoussis, E. (1992) *The Woburn Abbey collection of classical antiquities.* Monumenta Artis Romanae XX, Mainz, von Zabern.
Covel, J. (1722) *Some account of the present Greek church.* Cambridge, Crownfield.
Glaser, E. (2007) *Judaism without Jews: philosemitism and Christian polemic in early modern England.* Basingstoke, Palgrave Macmillan.
Rycaut, P. (1679) *The present state of the Greek and Armenian churches.* London.
Wheler, G. (1682) *Journey into Greece.* London, Cademan.

Depictions of Islam in Seventeenth-Century English Travel Accounts

Anders Ingram

The early seventeenth century saw a proliferation in English travel accounts describing the Levant, Holy land and Egypt. This was influenced by several factors, the foremost of which was the booming English Levant trade, which led to the establishment of regular trade routes as well as consuls and factories, and thus greatly facilitated travel. Other contexts include the relative peace then prevailing in Europe (the end of Anglo–Spanish and Hapsburg–Ottoman conflicts), and a noted increase in works printed in English on the topics of Ottomans, the Levant and North Africa. Such 'travel accounts' had not yet settled into the conventionalised and familiar genre of 'travel literature'. Rather, the

accounts we will examine are more fluid, situated between earlier pilgrimage accounts and the later Grand Tour, and often touching upon diverse elements such as geography, history, political discourse, culture (or 'manners'), religion, antiquarianism and classical literature. Given this breadth of interests and the centrality of Islam to the history and contemporary state of these lands, it is unsurprising that the accounts of travellers are peppered with references to Islam across a broad range of contexts, from descriptions of the Ottoman state and its peoples to travel anecdotes.

The seventeenth-century English traveller in the Levant, Holy land and Egypt was presented with plenty of opportunity to reflect upon Islam. For example, Figure 1, taken from Sandys' *A relation of a Iourney begun An: Dom: 1610* (1632, 31), shows the Golden Horn in Constantinople. The view is from Galata, where the European embassies were situated, and shows Topkapı palace on the left and the Aya Sophia to the right. It is unusual to find an illustration of a mosque in contemporary English travel accounts. However, this is not just any mosque, but the former church Sancta Sophia, once the glory of Christendom and 'now conuerted to a mosque, and consecrate to *Mahomet* after a Diabolicall manner', as Sandys' contemporary Lithgow's *A most delectable and true discourse* put it (Lithgow 1616, 49). The Aya Sophia is situated next to the Sultan's 'Seraglio', the visible centre of Ottoman power and an object of fascination to contemporary Europeans. This mosque is described by many contemporary English travellers to Constantinople, satisfying their desire to engage with the Christian history of the landscape, and to offer pithy reflections upon the power of the Ottomans and sad decline of Christendom.

Figure 1. View of Topkapi Palace and Aya Sophia from Galata. *Sandys, G. (1632, 31). By kind permission of the Trustees of the National Library of Scotland.*

Although travellers might include passing references to Islam across a variety of contexts, many of their accounts also contain a section giving a short summary of Islam's history and supposed character, supplemented by the authors' observations of contemporary Muslim life as they saw it. Such sections give a succinct summary of many of the images and assumptions underlying more anecdotal references to Islam, and as such provide the focus of this paper. The structure, attitudes and details of these descriptions are dominated by a deeply embedded Christian polemical tradition regarding Islam, which these authors took with them when travelling east. This paper will therefore begin with a brief outline of that Christian polemical tradition, before relating it to the accounts of several seventeenth-century English travellers, and finally examining how these travellers assimilated their experiences and observations of Islamic life and worship through these paradigms.

THE CHRISTIAN POLEMICAL TRADITION REGARDING ISLAM

Many scholarly accounts of the Christian polemical tradition regarding Islam have focused upon 'Islam and the West', to borrow Norman Daniel's phrase (Daniel 1960; Southern 1962; Frassetto and Banks (eds) 1999). However, the fundamentals of this tradition are present in the earliest Christian responses to Islam as far back as St. John of Damascus writing around AD 745 (Fletcher 2004, 23–8; Tolan 2002, 50–55). The second part of John's *Fountain of Knowledge*, a description of one hundred and one heresies, says of the 'superstition of the Ishmaelites'

> They are descended from Ishmael, was [*sic*, who] was born to Abraham of Agar, and for this reason they are called both *Agarenes* and *Ishmaelites*. They are also called *Saracens* ... a false prophet named Mohammed has appeared in their midst. This man, after having chanced upon the Old and New Testaments and likewise, it seems, having conversed with an Arian monk, devised his own heresy. (Chase trs. 1958, 153)

Beginning with a biblical genealogy of the 'Saracens' as Old Testament 'Ismaelites', John classifies Islam as a heresy and gives a polemical biography of the Prophet's life. This biography mocks and reviles various Islamic doctrines by relating them to the Prophet's supposed vices, and accuses him of cobbling together disparate elements of Judaism and Christianity with the help of a heretical Christian monk. These elements of heresy and polemical biography, alongside explanations of Islamic conquest and expansion rooted in eschatology and divine punishment, are the foundations of the Christian polemical tradition. Note that the origins of this tradition are not therefore 'western' in any meaningful sense; rather it has its roots in a broader 'Christian' reaction to the genesis of Islam.

Later, medieval European writers assimilated the details and arguments of earlier Eastern and Iberian Christian works on Islam, and crystallised them into highly set and generic form for a Latin Christian audience. The twelfth-century Cluniac works, written at the behest of Peter the Venerable, have often been highlighted as a key moment in this process (Daniel 1960; Southern 1962; Frassetto and Banks (eds) 1999). They included Robert Ketton's Latin translation of the Koran, Peter of Toledo's translation of the Arabic Christian apologetic work *Risâlat al- Kindî*, and two Latin polemical works by Peter of Cluny himself. The medieval influence of these texts is debatable; Mark of Toledo, a thirteenth-century Latin translator of the Koran, had not heard of Ketton's translation and believed he was the first to attempt such a task (Fletcher 2004, 129; Tolan 2002, 165). However, these texts proved to be of enduring significance and they were reprinted in the sixteenth century.

Ketton's Koran was reprinted in Basel in 1543, at the request of the Protestant divine Theodore Bibliander, and Luther himself supported both this publication and that of Peter of Cluny's two anti-Islamic polemics (Clark 1984, 3–13). Works such as Bibliander's Koran and Luther's *On war with the Turks* (*Vom Kriege Wider die Türken*, 1529) were a direct response to rapid and seemingly unstoppable Ottoman military expansion. This seemed particularly urgent following the collapse of the kingdom of Hungary following Ottoman victories at Belgrade in 1521, Mohács in 1526 and Buda in 1541. Writers such as Luther mobilised a long-established Christian polemical tradition, presenting Islam as divine punishment, as a vehicle for Reformation debates (Housley 2002, 85–96).

The first English works to deal with the Ottomans in any detail (also in the 1540s) heavily reflect this reformist agenda. For example, Bibliander's *A Godly consultation vnto the brethren and companyons of the Christen religion* (1542, an English translation from the Latin) follows his medieval sources and the reformist position. Thus it presents a biblical genealogy of the 'Saracens', treats Islam as a heresy, and includes a polemical biography of 'Mahumet' as a heresiarch who associates with heretical monks, supports his revelation with false miracles, and is given to epilepsy and sexual incontinency (Bibliander 1542, Sigs. C7v-D5r). Bibliander treats the Turks/Islam as a scourge sent to punish Christian vice, and his solution is a godly Reformation.

The history of Christian reactions and writing about Islam is of course far longer and more complex than the brief outline presented above. I have chosen to highlight these three periods in order to emphasise that the depictions of Islam in seventeenth-century travel accounts, to which we shall now turn, are not 'Orientalism' in Edward Said's sense of a discourse primarily shaped by 'western' domination of the 'east' (Said 1978). Rather, these travel authors mobilised a polemical tradition with its roots in a much broader *Christian* reaction to Islam, one recently reinvigorated by Ottoman power in Europe and Reformation responses to it.

PARADIGMS FOR ISLAM IN TRAVEL ACCOUNTS: ISLAM AS HERESY

Seventeenth-century travel accounts describing the Levant, Holy land and Egypt commonly contain a short summary of Islam, depicting its history, character, and tenets, enlivened by the authors' observations of the worship and 'manners' of the Muslim lands through which they had travelled. The underlying logic of such accounts is generally dictated by the Christian polemical tradition outlined above. A typical example is William Biddulph's *The trauels of certaine Englishmen* (1609), which begins it section on Islam, 'Wherfore, that I may the better make knowen vnto you their Religion, I will begin with the first Author thereof, which was (no doubt) the Deuill, who vsed that false Prophet *Mahomet* as his instrument to broach it abroad.' (Biddulph 1609, 46)

The structure and details of this account are typical. The fundamental assumption here is that Islam is a heresy i.e. authored by the devil and propagated by a false prophet. Biddulph, a churchman, explains the rise of Islam as the fulfilment of the Biblical prophecy of Daniel. He then swiftly moves to a polemical biography of 'Mahomet', followed by a summary of his understanding and observations of 'the religion of the Turkes', including the profession of faith, prayer, absolution, alms, fasting, marriage customs, and law. There is no sense of separation between Islamic law and Ottoman law and custom.

Biddulph's contemporary George Sandys begins his account of Islam with a biography of 'Mahomet the saracen law giuer'. I shall quote this at length as it is a particularly comprehensive roll call of contemporary views of Islam and its Prophet.

> Two yeares together he [Mahomet] liued in a caue, not farre distant from *Mecha*; where he compiled his damnable doctrine, by the helpe of one *Sergius* a *Nestorian* Monke, and *Abdalla* a Iew: (containing a hodgepodge of sundry religions;) ... His new religion by little and little he diuulged in *Mecha*; countenanced by the powerfull alliance which he had by his sundry wiues; and followed by many of the vulgar, allured with the libertie thereof, and delighted with the noueltie...
>
> Meane of stature he was, & euill proportioned ... Being much subiect to the falling sicknesse [epilepsy], he made them beleeue that it was a propheticall trance; and that he conuersed with the Angell *Gabriel*. Hauing also taught a Pigeon to feed at his eare, affirming it to be the holy Ghost, which informed him in diuine precepts ... so he drew the grosse *Arabians* to a superstitious obedience. For he had a subtill wit, though viciously employed; being naturally inclined to all villanies: amongst the rest, so insatiably lecherous, that he countenanced his incontinency with a

law: wherein he declared it, not onely to be no crime to couple with whom soeuer he liked, but an act of high honor to the partie, and infusing sanctitie. Thus planted he his irreligious religion, being much assisted by the inequities of those times: the Christian estate then miserably diuided by multitudes of heresies ....Which enlarging, as the *Saracens* and *Turks* enlarged their Empires, doth at this day wel-nigh ouer-runne three parts of the earth; of that I meane that hath ciuill inhabitants... (Sandys 1615, 53)

Sandys casts 'Mahomet' as the classic heresiarch, complete with false miracles, sexual deviancy and even 'witchcraft'. As an 'irreligious religion', 'Mahometanism' is presented as a parody or inversion of 'true religion' i.e. Christianity, and ascribed characteristics through this logic. Thus if Christianity is a spiritual religion of martyrs and tribulation, Islam is a worldly and sensual religion propagated by the sword and false miracles, and cynically designed to appeal to men's desire for power, wealth and carnal satisfaction. Islam's flawed doctrines and irrationality follow naturally from the physical, moral and spiritual infirmities of its false prophet (epilepsy, lechery etc.).

While Sandys' account seems violently abusive to the modern eye, it was typical of its time. The majority of these descriptions are highly generic, following the same format and repeating similar details. For example, his contemporaries Biddulph (1609) and Lithgow (1616) provide virtually identical biographies of a Mahomet born to a 'base' mixed Jewish and Arab parentage, given to both epilepsy and all manner of vices, who patches together a mix of heresy and cynicism with the help of an Arian monk named 'Sergius' (who Sandys made a Nestorian). Lithgow, a staunch Protestant with a deep hatred of Roman Catholicism, makes this 'Sergius, an *Italian* Monke', a comment which he removes from later editions (Lithgow 1616, 53). Lithgow's account probably drew on Biddulph's. Compare their descriptions of 'Mahomet' and 'Sergius': 'Héereupon these two helhounds ... patched vp a particular doctrine vnto themselues ... they brought foorth a monstrous and most diuellish Religion.' (Biddulph 1609, 48) 'heereupon these two hell-hounds ... patched vp a most monstruous and deuillish Religion to themselues, and to their miscreant beleeuers.' (Lithgow 1616, 54)

Polemical biographies of 'Mahomet' such as these are so similar and generic in character that it is very hard to establish their sources with any certainty. Lithgow and Biddulph may have shared a third mutual source. Further, the format and detail of such biographies was common beyond travel accounts. The geographer John Pory's *Africa* (1600, 380–7) includes a virtually identical description, as does the Samuel Purchas' giant cosmology *Purchas his Pilgrimage* (1613, 199–205); while the period's most influential English work on the Ottomans, Richard Knolles' *General History of the Turks* (1603) uses very similar language to depict 'the false Prophet *Mahomet*, borne in an vnhappie houre, to the great destruction of mankind: whose most grosse and blasphemous doctrine [was] first phantasied by himselfe in Arabia, and so by him obtruded vnto the world' (Knolles 1603, Sig Aiv[r]). All these authors simply regurgitate names, concepts and images drawn from the established Christian polemical tradition regarding Islam.

The schema of Islam as a heresy and 'Mahomet' as a heresiarch leads many early modern authors to treat it as an inverted or parodied version of Christianity. This tendency is comically evident in Lithgow's description of the architectural form of mosques:

> The Turkes haue no bels in their Churches, neither the vse of a clocke, nor numbring of houres; but they haue high round Stéeples, *for they contrafact and contradict all the formes of Christians* [my italics]; when they goe to pray, they are called together by the voyce of crying men, who go vp on the bartizings of their Stéeples, shouting and crying with a shrill voyce: *La illa, Eillala, Mahomet Rezul alla,* that is, *God is a great God, and Mahomet is his Prophet, or otherwise there is but one God.* (Lithgow 1616, 50)

Lithgow's understanding of Islam as a heresy, and therefore an inversion of Christianity, provides him with an explanation of the differences between the forms of churches and mosques ('they contrafact and contradict all the formes of Christians'). However, this highly pejorative schema does not prevent him from giving a fairly detailed description of some of the surface aspects of Islamic worship, in this case an accurate translation of the Islamic profession of faith and the observation that it is part of the call to prayer.

While the authors quoted here all gave first-hand accounts of Islamic worship in varying detail, none of them were led to question the paradigms through which they understood Islam. A further example is the churchman Thomas Smith, who served as a Levant company chaplain at Constantinople between 1668 and 1671. Smith was not an ignorant man; he was highly educated and spoke Arabic, Greek, Hebrew and Turkish. His *Epistolæ duæ, quarum altera de moribus ac institutis Turcarum agit* (1672) includes a reasonably lengthy glossary of terms giving translations in Arabic, Turkish and Latin. This work was later translated into English as *Remarks upon the manners, religion and government of the Turks* (1678). However, Smith's experiences in the Levant did not lead him to question the paradigms through which he understood Islam. In a section surveying the churches of Asia, Smith ruminates on the ruins of Ephesus:

> That which affected me with the deepest anguish and most sorrowful resentment when I was upon the place, and does still, was and is a reflexion upon the threat made against *Ephesus* mentioned in the second Chapter of the *Revelations* of St. John, who made his abode in that City, and died there. *Remember from whence thou art fallen, and do the first works: or else I will come unto thee quickly, and will remove thy Candlestick out of its place, except thou repent.* And upon a farther and more serious consideration, as I sorrowfully walked through the ruines of that City especially, I concluded most agreeably, not only to my function, but to the nature of the thing … that the sad and direful calamities which have involved these *Asian* Churches,

> ought to proclaim to the present flourishing Churches of *Christendom* (as much as
> if an Angel were sent express from Heaven to denounce the judgment) what they
> are to expect, and what may be their case one day, if they follow their evil example
> … and that their security lyes not so much in the strength of their frontiers, and
> the greatness of their armies, (for neither of these could defend the *Eastern Christians*
> from the invasion and fury of the *Saracens* and *Turks*) as in their mutual agreements,
> and in the virtues of a Christian life. (Smith 1678, 274–6)

Smith's identification of '*Saracens* and *Turks*' as the scourge of God and his
emphasis upon spiritual purity as the only defence from God's anger draw on
the long-established Christian response to Islam, which had been applied to the
Ottoman context in the previous century by Luther and his contemporaries.
Indeed, despite three years living in the Levant, Smith's views would not have
been out of place in mid-sixteenth-century Europe.

Smith's section on Islam includes detailed observations of Islamic worship,
assisted by his knowledge of Arabic and Turkish (including a number of short
'Arabic prayers'), alongside the usual elements of a polemical biography of the
Prophet, a summary of Islam's essential points of disagreement with Christianity,
and the portrayal of Islam as 'worldy' (i.e. sensual, salacious, violent and politic).
Although his observations were detailed, they never led him to question his own
paradigms. He approached Islam already certain of the truth and validity of the
venerable Christian polemical tradition regarding it, and therefore saw no reason
or need to delve deeper or engage with its ideas.

The Christian polemical tradition was such a fundamental part of English
views of Islam that it could even shape the views of those who consciously tried
to take a more open-minded view. Henry Blount's *Voyage into the Levant* (1636)
stated his rationalistic aim as 'to observe the Religion, Manners, and Policie of
the *Turkes* … (to wit) whether to an unpartiall conceit, the *Turkish* way appeare
absolutely barbarous, as we are given to understand, or rather an other kinde
of civilitie, different from ours, but no lesse pretending' (Blount 1636, 2). Blount
does not at any point describe Islam as diabolically inspired; neither does he
proceed via the familiar polemical biography of Mahomet. Rather, he abandons
the usual generic elements emphasised by English accounts of Islam, in favour
of a 'politicke' or indeed cynical interpretation:

> Now followes their *Religion*, wherein I noted only the *Politicke* institutions thereof
> … … for hee [Mahomet] finding the *Sword* to be the foundation of *Empires*, and that
> to manage the Sword, the rude and sensuall are more vigorous, then wits softned
> in a mild *rationall* way of *civilitie*; did first frame his *institutions* to a rude and insolent
> *sensuality*. (Blount 1636, 77–8)

In addition to the sword and sensuality, Blount emphasises the utility and
cynicism of Islamic doctrines, which indulge, or restrain, human desires for
'politick' ends.

> The cunning of that seconding [of] humane inclination appeares in the different
> success of two politick acts of the *Alcoran*: the one permits *Poligamie*, to make a
> numerous People, which is the foundation of all great *Empires:* The other pretending
> a divell in every grape, prohibits *wine*: thereby it hardens the Souldier, prevents
> disorder, and facilitates publique provision. (Blount 1636, 82).

While Blount neglects many of the images and details of standard contemporary
accounts of Islam, his portrayal of a 'politicke' Islam founded on the sword and
sensuality clearly draws heavily upon the familiar Christian polemical tradition.
Although he declares his impartial interest, his account is not so very far from
Biddulph's depiction of '*Mahomets Machiaueilian* deuices' (Biddulph 1609, 64).

In conclusion, many seventeenth-century English travellers' accounts of
journeys to the Levant, Holy land and Egypt provided short summary accounts
of Islam. Although these often included first-hand observations, of varying detail,
their underlying logic was dictated by the paradigms of a long-established
Christian polemical tradition. Not only did these travellers bring this tradition
with them as they voyaged eastward, but most of them probably also reinforced
it through wider geographical and historical reading as they wrote their accounts
upon their return. As a result, most of these accounts were highly generic,
revolving around a depiction of Islam as a heresy, followed by a polemical
biography of 'Mahomet', and then proceeding to an account of Islamic tenets,
worship, laws, customs and even 'manners' (where the boundary between Islamic
and Turkish blurs). Despite their at times detailed accounts of Islam, and lengthy
periods of travel or residence in Muslim lands, few of these travellers were led
to question what they already 'knew' from this tradition.

BIBLIOGRAPHY

Africanus, L. and trs. Pory, J. (1600) *A Geographical Historie of Africa*. London, Georg. Bishop,
   in Early English Books Online, http://gateway.proquest.com/openurl?ctx_ver=Z39.88–
   2003&res_id=xri:eebo&rft_id=xri:eebo:citation:99844139
Bibliander, T. (1542) *A Godly Consultation Vnto the Brethren and Companyons of the Christen
   Religyon*. Basill [i.e. Antwerp], Radulphe Bonifante [i.e. M. Crom], in Early English Books
   Online, http://gateway.proquest.com/openurl?ctx_ver=Z39.88–2003&res_id=xri:
   eebo&rft_id=xri:eebo:citation:99846912
Biddulph, W. (1609) *The Trauels of Certaine Englishmen*. London, W. Aspley, in Early English
   Books Online, http://gateway.proquest.com/openurl?ctx_ver=Z39.88–2003&res_id=xri:
   eebo&rft_id=xri:eebo:citation:99837764
Blount, H. (1636) *A Voyage into the Levant*. London, Andrew Crooke.
Chase, F. H. tr. (1958) *St. John of Damascus: Writings*. Washington D.C., Catholic University
   of America Press.

Clark, H. (1984) The publication of the Koran in Latin: A Reformation dilemma. *The Sixteenth Century Journal* 15:1, 3–13.

Daniel, N. (1960) *Islam and the West*. Edinburgh, Edinburgh University Press.

Fletcher, R. A. (2004) *The Cross and the Crescent*. London, Penguin.

Frassetto, M. and Banks, D. R., eds (1999) *Western Views of Islam in Medieval and Early Modern Europe*. Basingstoke, Macmillan.

Housley, N. (2002) *Religious Warfare in Europe, 1400-1536*. Oxford, Oxford University Press.

Knolles, R. (1603) *The Generall Historie of the Turkes*. London, Adam Islip.

Lithgow, W. (1616) *A most delectable and true discourse, of an admired and painefull peregrination from Scotland, to the most famous kingdomes in Europe, Asia and Affricke*. London, Thomas Archer, in Early English Books Online, http://gateway.proquest.com/openurl?ctx_ver=Z39.88–2003&res_id=xri:eebo&rft_id=xri:eebo:citation:99844242

Purchas, S. (1613) *Purchas his Pilgrimage*. London, Henrie Fetherstone.

Said, E. W. (1978) *Orientalism*. London and Henley, Routledge and Kegan Paul.

Sandys, G. (1615) *A Relation of a Iourney begun an: Dom: 1610*. London, W. Barrett.

Sandys, G. (1632) *A Relation of a Iourney begun an: Dom: 1610*. London, R. Allot.

Smith, T. (1678) *Remarks Upon the Manners, Religion and Government of the Turks*. London, Moses Pitt.

Southern, R. W. (1962) *Western Views of Islam in the Middle Ages*. Cambridge, Harvard University Press.

Tolan, J. (2002) *Saracens: Islam in the Medieval European Imagination*. New York, Columbia University Press.

Saved From Pirates

Peta Rée

When Sir Richard Worsley, Baronet, of Appuldurcombe on the Isle of Wight, set out on his travels in April 1783, his departure more resembled a flight than the beginning of an adventure. He had recently figured as plaintiff in a scandalous divorce, which had damaged his own reputation as much as that of his wife. Pursued in the public prints and scurrilous cartoons by well-deserved opprobrium, a strategic disappearance abroad seemed his only recourse.

At first he travelled only to Europe, but by early 1785 he had decided to venture further afield. We follow him here only on that 16-month long section of his travels which lay within ASTENE's sphere – Greece, Egypt and Turkey – and take leave of him as he heads off into Russia in June 1786. Even this must be but a series of snapshots, touching on a few particular incidents and observations, for his Journal, the source of this paper, is lengthy and detailed.

The entry for 11 February 1785 reads, 'Before my departure from Rome on my intended tour of Greece and Egypt, I engaged Mr Reveley, an English artist then at Rome to accompany me to make drawings of architecture and the most interesting Ruins.'

Swiftly passing Sicily, Malta and Crete, we join Sir Richard on 8 May, when he wrote exultantly, 'Towards Evening, to my irrepressible joy we had a sight of the Acropolis of Athens with the glorious temple of Minerva.'

About midday on the 9th they cast anchor in the Piraeus, 'since', noted Worsley, 'called Porto Lione, from two Lyons which formerly stood at the entrance of it where a chain was placed to prevent vessels entering the Harbour'. The 'extremely beautiful' road to Athens was bordered by vines and olive groves, in places by long-ruined walls. Sir Richard called on M. Gaspari, the French consul, and was gratified when he 'very obligingly insisted on my taking up lodgings in his house during my stay, there being no Hotels or Houses of Accommodation for Strangers'.

Athens, Worsley found, 'does not lie around the Acropolis as formerly, but on the north-east of it, surrounded with a high wall lately built by the present Governor with the fragments of many beautiful ruins'. The best house belonged to the Governor, any other good houses to the principal Athenians, some of whom had made their fortunes by trading in oil with French merchants. Even these houses were 'slightly built of wood and mortar', surrounded by a court and roofed with a dark reddish tile, which Sir Richard judged to give the city 'as viewed from the distance a very disagreeable appearance', somewhat mitigated by the several gardens and fountains disposed about the town.

'Athens, as it is natural to suppose,' noted Worsley, 'abounds in curious monuments of antiquity' – and not all in their original positions, for 'there is scarcely a house belonging to an Athenian that has not some small fragment of sculpture over the Door or in the Court'.

The Acropolis, of course, was Worsley's premier goal, but it was 'only with difficulty that the Turkish Governor permits Christians to the fortress to inspect and admire the surprising ruins it contains'. Xerxes' putting to fire of the original temple of Minerva 'has probably deprived us of an insight into the origin of Greek architecture', regretted Worsley, '[but] the august remains of the present Temple' 'most fully repaired this loss'. Mr Reveley soon made 'four stained drawings' of it 'on the spot with diligence and fidelity'.

After but five days, Sir Richard left him to get on with it, and departed to visit some of the islands, and then the Peloponnese. At Megara, he fell in with a M. Danson de Villoisons, who was searching for ancient inscriptions for the Society of Belles Lettres in Paris. 'At such a spot it was natural to become soon acquainted', and they continued their tour together.

Corinth, 'anciently famous for abounding with courtesans', was a scattered city, the houses so interspersed with fields and gardens as to resemble three or four contiguous villages rather than a 'grand City'. In Argos, they lodged at a large 'can' erected by the sister of the grand Signior. It was the handsomest building in a town otherwise consisting of about 450 low houses, two mosques and three Greek churches. At Nauplia, then called Napoli di Romana, there was a beautiful kiosk and public fountain enclosed in a garden, built by the 'great Admiral Hassan'. At Tripolissa they stayed with the Archbishop, 'who appears to be an enlightened man', then proceeded to Sparta, guarded by three soldiers, as it 'was by no means safe to travel in the Morea without them'.

They arrived back in Nauplia on 28 May, just as the town gates were closing – 'where we found the most melancholy sight imaginable. Three men had been impaled ... on a pretence of their being Laconian robbers and they were exposed naked upon the stakes to the view of the public.' Though executed two days before, the Pasha had not allowed them to be taken down and buried by their relatives, 'who always pay the Turks handsomely, to have the bodies. I never saw a sight more truly disgusting'.

Taking to the sea again, after a pause at Egina, they were back in Athens on 3 June. The Gasparis and Reveley, who had been drawing industriously, impatiently awaited Worsley, as a week later, joined by the English consul, they were to take a jaunt into the countryside and to Marathon.

On their return, they found Athens in an uproar, occasioned by the replacement of the Governor. On 24 June, Worsley suffered a personal disturbance when an earthquake shook his room 'very considerably'. The ceiling, which was old and made of wood. 'made a noise as if it was falling'.

At an evening party with the English consul, Worsley watched 'the Greek dance executed by young Athenians of the greatest distinction'. He describes something very similar to Greek folk dancing today, except that the women's hands could only be held by their parents. Worsley thought the idea of M. Le Roi 'very pretty', that 'there was an analogy between this dance and that mentioned by Plutarch, danced in Delos, and supposed to represent windings of the labyrinth'.

On 1 July, 'having finished the necessary drawings', he tore himself away from Athens 'with the greatest regret', and boarded his ship, the Aurora, bound for Egypt.

He paused some days on Mykonos, lodging with the Russian consul, Count Vonovich. Worsley, always interested in dress, had been much taken with some of the ladies' costumes he saw in Greece. By that of the otherwise handsome 'common' women of Mykonos, he was rather taken aback. He describes in detail an ensemble of which various layers of shifts, stomachers and petticoats were liberally gold or silver belaced or embroidered. The sleeveless corselet bore pearls as well. 'The stockings', wrote the astonished Sir Richard, 'are of red silk, clocks and seams of gold ... (they) are full of wrinkles occasioned by their wearing four or five pairs over one another to make the legs look thick which is thought a great beauty.' Ending at the foot in velvet or silk slippers that covered only the toes, and at the head by a turban wound from a cloth 6–7 feet long and 18 inches wide, this outfit was presumably best wear, hardly appropriate for doing the washing-up. On a visit to the neighbouring islands with Vonovich, Worsley found the dress of the women of Naxos so peculiar that he attempted no description.

At Rhodes, his next destination, Sir Richard was informed that when the famous Colossus had fallen in an earthquake, the pieces were sold to a Jew, 'who employed nine hundred camels in removing them'. Between Rhodes and Alexandria, he was told, there lurked a pirate vessel, which 'had committed the most cruel piracy, taking some merchant ships, killing the ship's company and plundering the ships before sinking them'.

Huddled in close convoy with two other ships, he set forth with some trepidation on 24 July. A boy was kept constantly at the masthead on the lookout for suspect sails. With enormous relief, they greeted the view of the two 'Large

Mounts of Rubbish' behind Alexandria towards the end of the next day. Soon the castle and minarets could be seen, and at 8 am on 26 July they cast anchor in the New Port. This was much exposed to north and north-east winds, but the Old Port, 'one of the finest imaginable', was forbidden to Christian vessels. 'Except for the Ruins of Antiquity', Worsley found Alexandria 'to afford little amusement for the curious'.

As he stood on the mount of Pompey's Pillar (which Reveley measured), he commanded

> a view of the City and the Port to the North and on the South an immense Desert ... very extensive, level and sandy, it appears at a small distance like a collection of water, which seems to advance as you do, keeping always before you at a distance of about a quarter of a mile whilst the intermediate space appears all in a glow, occasioned by the trembling fluctuations of the vapours exhaled by the sun's powerful influence; it is likewise surprising to observe in what an extraordinary manner every object is magnified ... insomuch that a shrub appears like a tree.

Sir Richard seldom gives so eloquent a description of a scene – but it was his first desert and his first mirage.

His viewing of Alexandria's ruins occupied him but five days, then he sailed in a trading vessel to Rosetta, where he lodged overnight with M. Varsey, a French merchant, married to the English sister-in-law of the late Edward Wortley Montague. On 1 August, Worsley hired a 'convenient small cabin' on a Maggi, a boat, unlike his rather unstable conveyance from Alexandria, 'large and well-calculated for passengers and goods', and sailed for Cairo.

Landing at Boulac, they were conveyed on asses to the house of Carlo Rosetti, 'Consul General for Prussia and other powers', where they were lodged 'much to our satisfaction'. The indefatigable sightseeing began again.

They inspected Joseph's Well, Joseph's Divan and Joseph's Palace, at which last there was a 'considerable silk manufactory'. Worsley found the people at work 'embroidering in gold on a black silk of the covering for the Tomb of Mahomet which is annually sent from Cairo to Mecca by the caravan'. In other rooms of the Palace there was a Mint.

There were but few soldiers in the Castle, which would, Worsley judged, be incapable of 'resistance against artillery from the overlooking Moccatam hills'. Returning from a visit to the hills, they came to the Tombs of the Caliphs, still held in such veneration that Christians and Jews must alight from their asses to pass by, as 'an expression of their respect'.

Murad Bey's palace, old Cairo, the Nilometer, the slave market, were visited, and of course the Pyramids. Commented Sir Richard,

> after all that has been said, it is a mortifying consideration that the most durable works in architecture have been owing to ignorance ..."Who knows ... [Worsley

quoted Baron Tott] whether the invention of the Pyramids was not owing to the ignorance they were in, since they had not any other method for covering a great circumference before the art of arching, and that of employing columns to support a roof, were invented."

In *his* ignorance, Worsley considered the Sphinx to be a woman 'resembling an Ethiopian'.

As they returned to Giza, they found the Nile had spread so rapidly across the plain in the last 12 hours that they would soon have needed boats to cross it. Which might have been a mercy, for 'the heat of the sand on which we had walked for some hours was so great that it had not only burnt our slippers, but likewise the skin of the legs and feet began to peel off, attended by considerable pain'.

It was the time of the Inundation. On 15 August, Worsley had witnessed the opening of the canals into Cairo; these, full of water for about a hundred days, would then dry out and become 'a receptacle for all the rubbish of the town'.

Once the canals were full, within about half an hour small boats began to pass along them, and the Ezbekieh became a lake. From his viewpoint in the house of one of the French merchants, Worsley took at least as much interest in his glimpses of 'several very fine women' behind the lattices of the house opposite.

Two weeks later, at 7 am, he watched the departure of the pilgrim caravan for Mecca. He gives a fascinated description of the parade: richly ornamented horses, led or ridden, camels ornamented, camels loaded with merchandise, litters carrying the wives or concubines of Agas, the head cook of the commander of the caravan, and his underlings, on foot, with 13 camels loaded with 'kitchen furniture', camels carrying water in skins, Mamluks riding, guards, drums, the guide to the caravan across the desert, dressed 'in a whimsical manner, mounted on a very fine lamb', and the camel 'more beautiful than all the rest', completely covered in gold and silver ornaments and ostrich feathers, who bore the pall for Mahomet's Tomb. His minute description fills four pages of the Journal.

Since in Upper Egypt the Mamluke Beys were 'at odds', even war, with each other, Worsley was deprived of satisfying his 'very considerable curiosity' about that part of the country. He departed Cairo on 9 September and Alexandria eight days later, headed for Turkey.

His voyage, mainly up the coast of Asia Minor, was, except when their ship was blown off course, uneventful, and they cast anchor at Smyrna on 21 October. Smyrna's situation, 'being placed in the centre of the trade of the Levant is so advantageous that it is the first trading city in the Levant', observed Worsley.

> The city, though not very large is much better built than is generally the case in the Levant. The streets are better lighted, better paved and the houses likewise

better and more commoding than in the other cities of Asia. The principal and most beautiful street is inhabited by the Franks, it extends along the park and contains the richest Magazines in the city and perhaps in all Asia.

Mr Hayes, the British consul, was away, but Worsley dined several times with his wife and her sons, and was shown around by Mr Barker (presumably father or uncle to the John Barker who was to be a consul in Aleppo, then Consul General in Egypt). On 2 November they sailed for Turkey. Nine days later they passed the lighthouse of Gallipoli and entered the Sea of Marmara – only nearly to be blown back out by a storm in the Hellespont. It was, as always at the end of a voyage, that 'to our great Joy' they cast anchor under the city walls of Constantinople.

The first sight of the city was 'striking', but on closer view Sir Richard found the streets narrow, ill-paved and dirty and the wooden houses to have the 'meanest appearance', though interspersed here and there with a few 'majestic' buildings such as the Bazaar and the Caravanserai. The architecture of the mosques he declared

> by no means pleasing, yet they do not fail to make a great impression on the beholders by their magnitude and solidity. The Domes are well executed, and these, with the Minarets add much to both the beauty of the Mosques and the city. ... Santa Sophia is the most perfect of all the Mosques [but its exterior] had the appearance of being a mass of confusion.

Worsley lodged at Pera, possibly with the British Ambassador, Sir Robert Ainslie, and mingled with other distinguished members of the Frank community – which may have been one circumstance to induce him to spend more time in Turkey, seven months, than in Greece or Egypt.

One day he accompanied Baron Didier, the Dutch Ambassador, to his audience with the Grand Signior. First they were given a dinner, but this 'lasted a very few minutes, for as soon as a plate was put on the table, it was taken off again, which in fact caused me no regrets for there was nothing that could tempt me scarcely to eat'.

Then the audience. The Grand Signior was seated on a throne, like 'a modern bed', but ornamented with pearls, costly jewels, strings of gold, 'Ostridges' eggs' and feathers; on his left a gold inkstand, on his right the sword of state. The Grand Vizier, in robes of white satin, and the High Admiral, clad in green lined with sable, 'stood with their hands crossed before them, to the Emperor's right; on the left stood the Ambassador, and behind him his son, secretary, and the gentlemen who had accompanied him to the audience. The Ambassador had only a side view of the Emperor, who never condescended to look at him.'
The Ambassador began his discourse, about friendship etc, which was interpreted by the Emperor's Greek Dragoman, standing

in a most humiliating posture, with his body bent forward, in which situation he continued during the whole ceremony; he was pale and trembled the whole time, which he had reason to do, as a word ill-paced or an improper look on the occasion would probably cause his head to be struck off at the Door of the Presence Chamber.

Then the Grand Signior signed to the Vizier by a nod to reply. The whole ceremony lasted rather more than a quarter of an hour, after which the Ambassador and his party returned to the Dutch Embassy for a proper dinner.

That was on 29 November. On 2 January 1786, Worsley went with Sir Robert Ainslie to the Arsenal, to visit the Captain Pasha, who had been appointed Caimakan by the Grand Signior upon the exile of the Vizier a few days before. Such was job security at the Ottoman court.

They were received cordially and shown the Treasury, at the door of which was a lion, which, chained at night, was loose in the daytime. 'The Lyon is tame, obeys his master and the Person who has care of him, but he has been known to show his character and a willingness to attack Europeans at times.' (As an aside, once when the French Ambassador was at a conference with the Captain Pasha, the lion approached and put its head in his lap. With admirable sang-froid indeed, he merely murmured 'Il est beau, fort beau', and carried on with his conversation.)

The Vizier's position was not the only insecure one in Turkey. Worsley remarked that

> due to the Turkish attitude to foreign ministers and unreliability in any treaty, it is … the indispensible duty of the Christian ambassadors to keep up a social union and intercourse … independent of the different political views of their respective Courts, for their own personal safety and the dignity of their characters.

Had that been so at the start of the recent Russo-Turkish war, 'the Turkish Ministry would not have dared to have sent the Russian resident to the Seven Towers'.

In April, Worsley made a three-week trip into Asia Minor, ruin hunting. He and Willey Reveley had fallen out irrevocably in Constantinople, and the artist accompanying him is not accorded a name, but is merely 'my Draftsman'.

Back in Constantinople by 5 May, Sir Richard accompanied Ainslie to watch the Turkish fleet sail for Egypt under the command of the Captain Pasha. 'No sooner was the fleet out of sight, but that the city, was in flames, which is a practice adopted by the People to show their disapprobation of some act of Government.'

It was time for Worsley too to depart. On 21 May he boarded a Russian sloop of war which the Russian envoy had ordered to take him to the Crimea. Delayed awaiting a fair wind, it was eight days before the customs officer came aboard to search – not for any of the many antiquities Worsley was carrying off, but for contraband of a very particular nature.

'I had purchased (a slave) of a Turkish Aga, who had been stole in Abyssinia, brought to Cairo and there sold and sent to Constantinople.' Under Turkish law, a ship found carrying a slave was forfeit. But 'they did not pretend to make a regular search', and did not find the boy concealed under the hatches. Unhappily for him, since Worsley was later remarked upon as treating the lad with 'barbarous cruelty'.

On 7 June 1786, Worsley saw the mountains of the Crimea rising above Balaclava, and, as he sets off into Russia, we shall bid him goodbye.

Sir Richard's manuscript Journal, now in the Lincolnshire Archives, is in two volumes. His neat small writing has the appearance of being more legible than it is. The pages are neither stained nor torn. This pristine condition is remarkable, considering what the manuscripts have been through.

You may be wondering why I have titled this paper 'Saved from Pirates'. You have heard warnings of pirates, of pirates being feared and watched out for, but no pirate has actually made an appearance. I must now confess to you that it was not Sir Richard who was saved from Pirates, but his Journal.

On the first page of each volume, in another hand than his, is written:

> This volume, along with several others effects, belonging to the Right Honourable Sir Richard Worsley, Bart., lately His Majesty's Resident in Venice, was captured on board an English ship bound for London in the year 1800, by a French privateer and carried into this Port, where the whole Property was concessed and sold. It fell into my hands by purchase from the person to whom it was originally adjudicated.
>
> Malaga 8th November 1805
(Signed) Duncan Shaw

Sir Richard was dead by November 1805, so it would appear Shaw returned his Journal to his heiress, who had married into the Yarborough family of Lincolnshire, and it was by them eventually given to the Lincolnshire Archives.

BIBILIOGRAPHY

Manuscript
Lincolnshire Archives: Worsley 23 and 24.

Publications
Ingamells, J. (1991) *A Dictionary of British and Irish Travelers in Italy*, compiled from the archive of Brinsley Ford, Paul Mellon Centre for Studies in British Art. London, Yale University Press.
Mansell, P. (1995) *Constantinople, City of the World's Desire, 1453-1924.* London, John Murray.
Rubenhold, H. (2008) *Lady Worsley's Whim.* London, Chatto and Windus.
The Oxford Dictionary of National Biography. Oxford, Oxford University Press.

Willey Reveley and the Greek Revival:
A Journey Through Italy, Egypt and Greece in the Years 1785 and 1786

Patricia Usick

In February 1785, Willey Reveley left Rome as self-described 'architect and draftsman' to Sir Richard Worsley for a journey through Italy, Greece and Egypt to Constantinople. While Worsley was seeking refuge from the scandal of his divorce after a lengthy stay in Spain and Portugal, for Reveley, like many architects of his generation, a trip to Rome to study the ancient remains was deemed essential, Rome then being regarded as the great model of classical architecture. The pair may have been perfectly matched in their interests, as

Figure 1. The Castle of Otranto. *Watercolour by W. Reveley. © The Trustees of The British Museum.*

Worsley was an important promoter of the Greek Revival in architecture through his two-volume *Museum Worsleyanum* (1794–1803) and Reveley, by his early death in 1799 aged only 39, had merited the title 'The Athenian Reveley' through his uncompromising editing of the third volume of the influential *Antiquities of Athens* (1762) by James 'Athenian' Stuart and Nicholas Revett. By temperament, however, the combination of the travellers was to prove disastrous, and they were to part on bad terms, in Constantinople in 1786.

Reveley, whose first name derived from his mother being the heir of Robert Willey of Newby Wiske, trained under the architect Sir William Chambers and was admitted to the Royal Academy Schools in 1777. He became assistant clerk of works at Somerset House, a Chambers' project, in 1781–2 (Hind). Although few of Reveley's architectural designs were built, his plans were wide ranging and included churches, a Gothic chapel, a mansion and hothouse, a palace, a mausoleum to Handel, bridges, chimney-pieces, a villa, a hospital, and a music theatre.

Reveley left a manuscript journal of their travels (RIBA BAL, MS Re W/1, fols. 165–88). It begins in Rome as they set off in their carriage at half past seven on the morning of 12 February 1785. The weather was subject to violent changes, but as they moved south through the villages of Campania he found the countryside abundant 'with olive, orange, lemon, bay and myrtle trees'. They stopped to record anything of architectural, and especially Greek, interest. Driving towards Naples, Reveley found the inns 'wretched', the beds 'of straw, & full of bugs', the food 'so filthily dressed that it turned our stomachs', the tavernas 'miserable', the ferry 'ill-contrived', the air 'bad', the people 'unhealthy', and the wine 'execrable'. South of Naples they stopped at Paestum and Reveley made two large watercolour drawings of the temples of Ceres and Neptune: Greek temples on Italian soil. Due to the lawlessness of Puglia they merged their two carriages into a convoy of five, including five priests, 'one of whom seemed fitter for a brothel than a church', and an old woman 'who had an ingenious way of leaning out of the cales & watering the road without detaining us by getting out, as any other person would have done...'

They reached the coast at Brindisi, where Reveley sketched the capital of the column of Augustus which marks the end of the Appian Way. At nearby Otranto, he drew the Castle 'so celebrated in Mr Walpole's novel'. From there they cruised along the coast of Sicily to Malta, where they were quarantined. Sailing towards Crete, Reveley 'vomited continuously', not seasick but very ill from a fever during the passage. Things hardly improved in Crete, where the climate and government were deemed 'terrible', the city unsafe, and the inhabitants 'the most lying, thieving, execrable wretches possible to imagine'. They sailed again on 1 May, stopping at Cape Colonna (formerly Souniam) to plan the Temple of Minerva. On 9 May they reached the port of Piraeus for Athens. Worsley set out immediately on foot over the five miles to Athens, while Reveley followed on horseback the following day, still rather weak from his fever.

The following weeks were spent studying the Parthenon and the other remains on the Acropolis and around the city. On 11 June there was an excursion to Mount Hymettus in a large party with Mr Gaspery, 'a French Greek with the title of Agent' in whose house they were lodged, his wife, her sister Madame Miette, Mr Roque his brother-in-law, a Dr de Villoison, and Mr Macree, the English consul. They visited and recorded Marathon, examined Pendeli, the marble quarry which supplied the Parthenon, and saw ancient Eleusis. Worsley continued to purchase ancient gems and fragments, statues and reliefs, for his collection. Their admiration for Greek architecture was evidently confirmed in Athens and Reveley left the city 'with infinite regret'. A tour of the Cycladic islands followed, then Rhodes and Alexandria. The journal ends abruptly here, for no apparent reason, but we can continue to trace Reveley's travels through the titles of his topographical drawings, since he was in the habit of dating them and writing full descriptions on the verso. He also left a highly idiosyncratic manuscript for a *Dictionary of Architecture*, in which are found personal observations on monuments he had visited (RIBA BAL, MS Re W/1 fols 165–88).

We know from Worsley's journal that they sailed in to Alexandria on 26 July 1785 (Lincolnshire Archives: Worsley 23, 24). At Alexandria Reveley drew the new port and city and the ancient obelisks, visiting and recording the Catacombs and Pompey's Pillar. A view of Rosetta was made, en route to Cairo, where he made drawings of the Citadel, the island of Rhoda, the Nilometer, and the mosque of the Mamluk Sultan Zahir outside the Eastern Gate. At the pyramid fields he made views of Saqqara 'in the Plain of the Mummies' and Giza 'at sunset', where he drew the Great Pyramid and two views of the Sphinx. At ancient Heliopolis, he copied the hieroglyphic inscription on the obelisk. There is no evidence that Reveley had any great interest in ancient Egypt, as he and Worsley were intent on the Rediscovery of Greece and not the Rediscovery of Egypt. Their focus was the study of ancient Greek remains in Italy, the Greek mainland and islands, and Asia Minor.

Because of the unsettled political situation the pair were unable to journey up the Nile, where they would have encountered the remains of great temples known from the works of Norden and others. It was already July and the heat in Egypt must have been intense and uncomfortable. Almost all the monuments they encountered were Greco-Roman or Islamic, and Reveley left the description of the pyramids in his *Dictionary of Architecture* to a memorandum by Worsley, who mainly quotes from classical sources, while giving some rather far-fetched information from earlier travellers. Worsley does attempt some original thoughts on the nature of the ashlar facing at the top of the second pyramid, and both men were sceptical of earlier descriptions. They climbed the Great Pyramid and

Figure 2. The Mosque of Sultan Jahir, Cairo *(the mosque of the Mamluk Sultan Zahir in Husainiyya). Watercolour by W. Reveley.* © *The Trustees of The British Museum.*

entered its passages, and examined the Sphinx, observing that it was cut out of the solid rock face 'in the exact character of an Ethiopian, the jaws being very prominent', the nose 'broken on purpose', and the strata of rock 'mouldered away'. Reveley's *Dictionary* entry for 'Egypt' is merely a potted history from classical sources, but he includes the so-called Labyrinth (actually the Fayoum mortuary temple of Amenemhet III) and comments on the architecture of the (unvisited) temples of Upper Egypt.

From Egypt they travelled by ship up the coast of Asia Minor towards Constantinople, with Reveley making drawings along the coast. In Constantinople he drew the Mosque of Sultan 'Achmet', Santa Sophia and a view of the Bosphorus. Reveley, sickened by Worsley's treatment of him as a servant not a gentleman, left his employ in Constantinople, and Worsley went on to make an expedition to the coast of Asia Minor and Troy in April 1786, with an anonymous 'draftsman' who was not Reveley. (A gentleman could pick up a draughtsman on his travels much as one might today buy a camera.) Worsley travelled on to Russia, where he stayed for a couple of weeks at Krichev with the philosopher and social reformer Jeremy Bentham and his brother Samuel, the latter in the employ of General Potemkin, protégé and lover of Catherine the Great.

Bentham had landed in Constantinople in October or November 1785 to find Sir Robert Ainslie's spare room at the British Embassy already occupied by Worsley, Reveley, and the Hon. Mr Cadogan, who was on his way to Egypt. Worsley's notoriety preceded him. Bentham was aware that 'He had made himself ridiculous and celebrated by exhibiting his wife naked', and found him in person 'haughty, selfish and mean' (Bentham 1843, 153).

Moreover, Reveley had added considerably to Bentham's unfavourable opinion by accusing the baronet of 'ill-usage – that his commands were given in the style of a bashaw – in a word, that his dependants were in the situation of slaves in the presence of a depot; he even menaced them with the rod and scourge'. Worsley had in fact just purchased a slave, an Abyssinian boy whom, Bentham reported, '[h]e treated ... with barbarous cruelty'.

Reveley had returned to Rome by 12 February 1786, when he signed a receipt for the payment of his salary. Worsley had paid him £50 in Constantinople when he left, and a further £100 was paid to him in Rome on Worsley's account by Thomas Jenkins, the banker and antiquary, 'in full of all demands by me on the said gentleman for having accompanied him on his travels through Greece etc. to Constantinople, and for having finished all the drawings, having no demands on the said Sir Rd. Worsley on any account whatever'.

Reveley remained in Rome, where he met, and on 17 April 1788 married, Maria James, daughter of an English merchant in Constantinople, in whose house Jeremy Bentham had been a constant visitor, delighted by this charming, motherless girl, with whom he discussed literature and whose piano playing he accompanied on the violin. Maria was probably born in London but taken to Constantinople to live with her father when she was eight. Beautiful, talented and well read, in 1785, aged 15, she and her father moved to Rome, where she studied painting under Angelica Kauffman and was described as running wild with no proper chaperone by Mary Shelley, wife of the poet and later a close friend (Kegan 1876, I, 81). This led to the situation described by Elizabeth Cooper to George Cumberland:

> at eleven o'clock one evening Reveley had been caught *in flagrante* with Miss James by her father; the pair were obliged to run almost naked to the architect's lodgings, with the irate father in pursuit; the next night they were married by an English clergyman and, since her father would provide nothing, various ladies in Rome collected money to buy the unfortunate bride some clothes. (BL Add.36495, f.303 (25 March 1788) quoted in Ingamells 1979, 807)

Maria's father refused to help the couple financially, and Reveley had only his father's allowance of £140 a year. Maria gave up her studies and they had returned to London by October 1788, when he made his will. Back in London, Reveley, an enthusiastic political liberal with 'hopes and expectations of political freedom', became a friend of the political anarchist William Godwin and the writer and dramatist Thomas Holcroft. Holcroft was later put on trial for high treason for his views and Maria was terrified she and Reveley would be 'compromised' by his evidence. 'His treatment of Mr Reveley excites in me the most unpleasant feelings; I believe I shall ever think of it with detestation.' (Kegan 1876, I, 135)

Reveley is described as 'a man of great attainments in his science', who had 'followed the steps of Athenian Stuart in his travels' *(Gentleman's Magazine* 1799 (i), 627). 'His collection of drawings, universally known to all the lovers of art, and admirers of classical Antiquity', was made during his travels with Worsley 'till, on some difference they separated, and Mr R retained his own drawings, which he Afterwards exhibited to his particular friends'. His obituary, while praising his talents and lamenting his sudden and early death, attributed his career failures to his lack of tact in dealing with potential clients. Reveley had presented plans for a 'new arrangement of the public baths at Bath ... of great beauty and elegance, replete with convenience'. 'But this hope passed away, 'as Mr Reveley's hopes were very apt to do' since Reveley 'had rather an awkward way of letting loose his real opinions; and had habituated himself to a sarcastic mode of delivering them. It need not be added that such qualities were not calculated to render him popular.' Many prospective clients sought 'architects of more pliant and accommodating dispositions'. His search for work 'appears to have been continually baffled'. He lost the contract for a hospital in Canterbury for similar reasons. There were some successes: In 1792–5 the church of All Saints, Southampton, was built to his designs in a neo-classical style. (The church was destroyed by bombing in 1940.) In 1798 he completed a country house in Sussex, and possibly another the same year.

Evidence of Reveley's intemperate blasts can be found both in his journal and in the work for which he is perhaps best remembered. On his return, the irritable traveller has given way to the self-confident critic and advanced Greek Revivalist. Stuart and Revett's publication of *Antiquities of Athens* in 1762 was a siren call for the appreciation of ancient Greek architecture, and also, as its title implies, it created a new emphasis on archaeology, accurate measuring and sketching, and personal observation. More importantly, this new 'Gusto Greco' now threatened the supremacy of Roman architecture, not merely as a theoretical study of history, but by aiming to promote the copying of Greek detail in modern buildings. This resulted in the professional antipathy of James Stuart's rivals, Robert Adam, Chambers and Piranesi, none of whom had travelled to Greece. Adam's response to Stuart's use of Greek detail in the interiors of Spencer House, London, was the comment: 'Greek to the teeth, but by God they are not handsome'. However, even architects like Wyatt, Holland and Soane, who were sympathetic to the 'Gusto Greco', relied on the plates of *Antiquities* since none of *them* had travelled to Greece.

Following the death of James Stuart, Reveley was asked by his widow to edit the third volume of *Antiquities of Athens,* for which Stuart had prepared only scanty material: 'numerous memorandum books and loose papers'. Reveley was confident enough to include drawings, descriptions and comments based on his own study of Greek antiquity with Worsley 'on the spot'. Unfortunately, he also chose to devote virtually the entire preface to an attack on his former mentor, the eminent Sir William Chambers, surveyor-General to His Majesty's works, who had denigrated the 'Gusto Greco', declaring that 'one might with equal success oppose a Hottentot and a Baboon to the Apollo and the Gladiator as set up the Grecian Architecture against the Romans' and going on 'to ridicule Stuart and Revett in intemperate language'. Reveley pointed out that Chambers was 'contemptuous' of Greek art but had never visited Greece and

> The Reasonings of Sir William Chambers, if they can deserve the name, will be seen by architects of real knowledge in their true light ... Sir William seems to insinuate ... that the Parthenon would gain considerably with respect to beauty by the addition of a steeple. A judicious observer of the fine arts would scarcely be more surprised were he to propose to effect this improvement by adding to it a Chinese pagoda.

By comparison with *Antiquities of Athens*, Reveley's contribution to the prestigious volumes of the *Museum Worsleyanum* appears less significant. The book's contents are divided into six classes, consisting of illustrations and descriptions of sculpture, bas reliefs, gems etc. and including a series of engravings of the Parthenon sculpture attributed to William Pars. Drawings attributed to Reveley in the Soane Museum include a tracing of sketches of Metopes from the Parthenon and details from the Tower of the Winds, and it is unlikely that he did not prepare many similar drawings from other monuments in Athens, but they are not included. His drawings are found only in the final class: 'a select collection of Views and Ruins of ancient buildings in the Levant, and Lesser Tartary, engraved chiefly from drawings made on the spot, with great accuracy, by that ingenious artist Mr Reveley'. Even in this group there are drawings by Pars and Richard Chandler, and the Crimean drawings cannot be by Reveley, as we have seen.

It seems evident that there were two sets of drawings, one portfolio in Worsley's possession, the other, presumably copies made with the permission of his employer, with Reveley, although the whereabouts of many drawings remain unknown. In their day both portfolios were much admired (Reveley's papers contain a request from the connoisseur Charles Townley to bring some friends to view his 'valuable drawings', with an invitation back to dinner at Park Street afterwards). Worsley presented a copy of Reveley's 'coloured drawing of the Castle of Otranto' to Lady Craven in Constantinople with the request that it be passed on to her friend Horace Walpole, author of the Gothic novel of that name and a sharp critic of Worsley's behaviour (Craven 1789, 282). Walpole, apparently unaware that the drawing came from Worsley, was surprised, as 'when I wrote my fantastic tale I did not know that there existed, or ever had existed, a castle at that place, but looked into the map of Naples for a name, and adopted Otranto as well-sounding'. Indeed, the castle matched his own description so perfectly he doubted its authenticity, asking Sir William Hamilton to discover whether it had been conceived or adapted 'to flatter the vanity of the author' (Lewis 1937–80, vol. 35, 435–6). That drawing is annotated 'the real castle of Otranto', and Walpole had it engraved for later editions of his novel. In 1789, Walpole gave Reveley a personal tour of Strawberry Hill (Lewis 1937–80, vol. 12, 232n).

Worsley's portfolio of drawings and his collection of antiquities were proudly showed off, confirming his reputation as a scholar and connoisseur and dimming, he hoped, memories of his divorce proceedings and his infamous reputation as a cuckold and voyeur. At St Petersburg, Catherine the Great 'stayed two hours to see my drawings'. Later, the drawings were displayed for visitors in Venice, where Worsley had secured the position of British Minister-Resident in 1993. James Morritt and his friend, both 'Grecian travellers', were treated to a display of his cabinet of treasures, to which he had added masterpieces of paintings, culminating in his portfolio of Reveley's images which, Morrittt wrote, 'gave us a gallop on our own hobby horse through from the plains of Greece and Asia, of most of which he has good drawings'. But while Worsley digressed, Morritt 'could not help now and then thinking of the *peeping* scene', the evidence of a complaisant and voyeuristic husband, much lampooned in the popular press (Morritt 1985, 305).

In May 1797, Napoleon's troops advanced on Venice and Worsley hurriedly packed up his treasures and fled, depositing as much of his collection as he could remove in the Adriatic port of Fiume. Four years later, the ship returning his collections, including the original drawings for the *Museum Worsleyanum*, was seized by a French Privateer, taken to the port of Malaga and held hostage. The paintings were 'bought up' by Lucian Bonaparte and other antiquities were sent on to Paris, but Worsley paid the bounty for the remainder. In the 1804 inventory of Appuldurcombe House, Worsley's country seat, a portfolio of 200 drawings are listed (only some 20 of these, of Russia and probably Venice, are not by Reveley). At least two of Reveley's 'very large and fine coloured drawings' were displayed in the Athenian Room. After Worsley's death in 1805, his collections passed to his niece's family and had been entirely dispersed by 1863. By then his Greek marbles had been quite outshone by those of Lord Elgin. Worsley's portfolio was probably broken up; Reveley's was sold on his death. Two drawings turned up anonymously in a private Spanish library in 2008 (perhaps through the Malaga connection), and there are more drawings in the Soane Museum,

Figure 3. Arch of Trajan, Benevento. *Watercolour by W. Reveley.* © *The Trustees of The British Museum.*

the British Museum, the Royal Institute of British Architects, the Yale Center for British Art and the Victoria and Albert Museum. Albums of his early architectural designs were sold by Sotheby's and Christies in 1979 and 1982.

The posthumous sale catalogue of Reveley's possessions included many of the 'well-known topographical views and drawings' made on his travels. 'Mr Urban' of *The Gentleman's Magazine* regretted that 'the whole collection did not fall into one person's hands'. He purchased a few drawings, Mr Bowyer paid 28 guineas for the journal, and the 80 drawings made on Reveley's journey brought in some £250 (*The Gentleman's Magazine* 1801 (i), 419–20). Sir John Soane bought architectural volumes from Reveley's library, and a variety of drawings from Reveley's estate, including tracings, designs, sketches, and charming pencil portraits of the delightfully pretty young women Reveley had encountered on his travels: the pert Mlle Miette from Athens, a serious Miss Caterina Barazzapoula of Naxos, and Miss Marietta Pangola, daughter of the English Consul at Zea. Soane also purchased two colossal casts of a capital and cornice from the Temple of Castor and Pollux in the Forum: the ruin epitomised the apogee of Roman architecture and was frequently copied in miniature as a Grand Tour souvenir. Soane's own design for the Bank of England had not been immune from Reveley's criticism: his letter of 1796 complains the entablature conveyed 'impropriety, I had almost said absurdity', the column bases 'do you no credit...' but ends, perhaps optimistically, 'I do assure you upon my honour that I have not the least wish to injure, but rather add to your reputation'. It is possible that Reveley had hoped to obtain the commission himself.

On 6 July 1799, at his house in Oxford Street, aged 39, Reveley suffered, without warning, 'the breaking of a blood vessel on the brain... He became gradually stupefied, and his senses, one by one – first his taste, then his sight failed him.' Despite her admission that 'they had at time disagreed, and believed themselves unsuited to each other', Maria was greatly shocked by the manner of his death; they had shared 15 years and an adored son. She had always believed in his integrity and staunchly defended him.

Reveley was less an artist-traveller than an architect, and the result of his journey was not to be an illustrated travel book but the experience of returning to London as one of the few architects boasting a personal experience of Greek architecture. Worsley was to promote the portfolio, drawn 'on the spot', to his own advantage as a collector and connoisseur, and in so doing he provided Reveley with a reputation and position that others could not match. Reveley is only remembered today for his editing of the third volume of *Antiquities of Athens* and for a single church, now lost.

BIBLIOGRAPHY

Manuscripts
British Library Add. Mss. 46501, f.79.114
Lincolnshire Archives: Worsley 23 and 24
RIBA BAL, MS Re W/1, fols 165–88
Sir John Soane Museum, ADD6, Vol. 31 and casts M45 and M47.

Publications

Bentham, J. (1843) *The Works of Jeremy Bentham.* Edinburgh, William Tait.

Bolton, A. T. (1927) *The Portrait of Sir John Soane, RA.* Frome; London, Soane Museum Publications.

Colvin, H. (4th ed. 2008) *A Biographical Dictionary of British Architects 1600-1840.* New Haven, London, Yale University Press.

Craven, Lady E. (1789) *A Journey through the Crimea to Constantinople.* Dublin, H. Chamberlaine, etc.

Friedman, T. (2002) Willey Reveley's All Saints', Southampton, *Georgian Group Journal* 12.

Fuller, C. ed. (2000) *The Correspondence of Jeremy Bentham* vol. II, Jan 1822–June 1824. Letters 580, 590, correspondence iii. Oxford, Clarendon Press.

Hind, C. W. (2004) Reveley, Willey (1760–1799), *Oxford Dictionary of National Biography.* Oxford, Oxford University Press; online edition.

Ingamells, J. (1979) *A Dictionary of British and Irish Travellers in Italy, 1701-1800.* Compiled from the Brinsley Ford Archive by John Ingamells. New Haven, London, Yale University Press.

Kaloustian, D. (2004) Gisborne, Maria (1770–1836), *Oxford Dictionary of National Biography.* Oxford, Oxford University Press; online edition

Kegan, P. C. (1876) *William Godwin: his friends and Contemporaries,* 2 vols. Vol. I, 81, 135–6, 332, vol. II, 314. London, Henry S. King & Co.

Le Roy, J.-D. (1770) *Les Ruines des plus beaux monuments de la Grece, etc.* A Paris: de l'Imprimerie de Louis-Francois Delatour. Et se vend chez Musier fils, libraire, 2nd ed.

Lewis, W. S. (1937–80), *Horace Walpole's Correspondence.* Oxford, Oxford University Press.

Morritt, J. B. S., ed. G. E. Marandin (1985) *A Grand Tour: Letters and Journeys, 1794-6.* London, Century.

Nichols, J. (1815) *Literary Anecdotes of the Eighteenth Century,* ix. London, Nichols, Son and Bentley.

Papworth, W. ed. (1853–92) *The Dictionary of Architecture,* 11 vols. London, Architectural Publications Society.

Rubenhold, H. (2008) *Lady Worsley's Whim: An Eighteenth-Century Tale of Sex, Scandal and Divorce.* London, Chatto & Windus.

Stieglitz, C. L. (1798–1800), *Plans et desseins tires de la belle architecture.* Paris and Leipzig.

Stuart, J. and Revett N. (1794) *Antiquities of Athens* Vol. III. London.

The Gentleman's Magazine (1799), (i), 627; 1801 (i), 419–20; 1806 (i), 587.

Worsley, Sir R. (1804) *A Catalogue Raisonne of the Principal Paintings, Sculpture, etc. at Appuldurcombe House.* London, William Bulmer & Co.

James Rennell and his Scientific World of Observation

Janet Starkey

WHO WAS JAMES RENNELL?

In 1791 Fanny Burney (1854 5, 226–7) described Major James Rennell as

> full of characteristic intelligence, simply and clearly delivered; and made us all
> wiser by his matter, if we remembered it, and gayer by his manner, whether we
> remembered it or not. I hope to meet him often. He is a gay little wizen old man,
> in appearance, from the eastern climate's dilapidations upon his youth and health;
> but I believe not old in years, any more than in spirits.

The following year she mentioned that Rennell 'has a plain, unadorned way of
giving information, that is both pleasant and masterly' (Burney 1854–5, 300).
Mrs Alicia Bryne, in her account of the Thackeray family, described Rennell as
being 'of middle height, well proportioned, with a grave yet sweet expression
of countenance. He was diffident and unassuming, but ever ready to impart
information. His conversation was interesting, and he had a remarkable flow of
spirits. In all his discussions he was candid and ingenuous.' (Markham 1895,
171–2)

Major James Rennell FRS (1742–1830) was born near Chudleigh and brought
up there by a guardian, the Reverend Gilbert Burrington, his mother having been
widowed in 1747 (Vetch 2004). Rennell entered the Royal Navy as a captain's
servant in January 1756, just before the Seven Years' War with France. Four years
later he volunteered to go with Captain Hyde Parker (1714–82) to the East Indies
Station. Between 1760 and 1763 he saw some active service, including the capture
of Pondicherry from the French after it capitulated in January 1761. He became
such an expert in marine surveying that Parker lent his services to the East India
Company. He later transferred and undertook surveys under the highly talented
Alexander Dalrymple (1737–1808), who joined the East India Company in 1752
and became its first hydrographer in 1779. Dalrymple produced thousands of

nautical charts and also explored commercial possibilities and routes in South Asia; as part of this mission, Rennell accompanied Dalrymple to Sulu and was even left a prized sextant when Dalrymple died, broken-hearted at his dismissal, in 1808. In 1764, Rennell joined the Bengal Marine Service, commissioned as ensign in the Bengal Engineers, and arrived in Calcutta when Governor Henry Vansittart (1732–70), Robert Clive's successor as Governor of Bengal from 1759 to 1764, was planning a survey of Bengal. Owing to the friendship with Mr Topham, who had served with Rennell in the Navy and who afterwards became a civil servant in the Company, Rennell was appointed surveyor-general of the East India Company's dominions in Bengal from 1764. Over the next 13 years, he surveyed an area of about 300,000 square miles.

Figure 1. Major James Rennell F.R.S. 1799. Frontispiece, James Rennell (1830).

In 1772 Rennell married Jane Thackeray (1739–c.1820), great-aunt of the great novelist, William Makepeace Thackeray, who was born in Calcutta whilst his father Richmond was serving there. Jane was a daughter of Dr Thomas Thackeray (d.1760), headmaster of Harrow, who left a widow and 15 children. As a result, Jane was sent to Calcutta to join her brother, William Makepeace Thackeray, the grandfather of the novelist, where he worked in the Bengal Civil Service from 1765. This brother later became Secretary to John Cartier, the Governor of Bengal from 1769 to 1772. Rennell made his headquarters in Dacca (Dhaka) and formed many lasting friendships including Thomas Kelsall, Lady Clive's cousin, who served the East India Company for 18 years in India from 1754, Cartier, and Major-General Claude Martin, an eclectic French Indophile employed by Nawab Asaf-Ud-Daula of Oudh (Markham 1895, 47). Other close lifelong friends were Dr Francis Russell, the station surgeon, and Sir Hugh Inglis, a commission merchant who then traded in Calcutta, where he made a fortune. Inglis was elected East India Company Director in 1784, made a baronet in 1801 and thrice served as Chairman and Deputy Chairman of the East India Company. Inglis warmly supported the accumulation of material on the history and culture of the East. Both Inglis and Francis Russell were, coincidentally, cousins of Dr Patrick Russell MD, formally of Aleppo and editor of the second edition of the *Natural History of Aleppo* (1794), his brother

Alexander's classic book with the same title (1756). Patrick also served in the Carnatic and later became a close friend and neighbour to Rennell in London.

Injured by Sanusi in 1776 in a skirmish on the frontiers of Bhutan, Rennell was brought by open boat 300 miles to Dacca, where he was treated by Dr Francis Russell. He never fully recovered. He retired as a major of the Bengal Engineers in 1776 at the age of 35 and was later granted a pension of £600 per annum by Sir Warren Hastings. From 1777 until his death in 1830, Rennell stayed in London, where he spent most of his time researching, chiefly among the materials and travel narratives in East India House, including the Orme Manuscripts, originally bequeathed in 1801 by the East India Company historiographer, Robert Orme. A prolific writer, Rennell's interests did not lie only in India or in his ground-breaking oceanographic studies but also in travelogues in the Middle East and North Africa. Although he never travelled in the region, Rennell was a scholar who deserves a place in this book for several reasons, as this paper will explain.

HIS LONDON CIRCLE

First, on his return to London, from 1777 Rennell lived at 23 Suffolk Street (later called Nassau Street), which was not far from that of his great friend and mentor, the President of the Royal Society, Sir Joseph Banks (1743–1820), who lived at 32 Soho Square, and both establishments became meeting places for a great network of travellers. In 1809, his talented daughter Jane married Admiral Sir John Tremayne Rodd KCB, and lived in Wimpole Street. His 'old messmate, Topham, lived in Queen Street, Berkeley Square', whilst

> [h]is Dacca friends, Kelsall, Hugh Inglis, Dr. Francis Russell, and his brother-in-law Harris, were all in England, and often in London. His wife's connections were numerous … an intimacy soon sprang up between him and the President, Sir Joseph Banks; Dr. Vincent, the Head Master of Westminster, and the author of the 'Voyage of Nearchus' and the 'Periplus of the Erythraean Sea' [1809]. Among his other intimate friends, who were also neighbours, were Sir Everard Home and Dr. John Hunter the great physicians, Alexander Dalrymple the hydrographer, and William Marsden the historian of Sumatra and editor of 'Marco Polo' [1818]; and Lord Spencer and Lord Mornington (afterwards Marquis Wellesley) in later years. Another very intimate friend was Dr. John Gillies, the Historiographer of Scotland, who, like Sir Joseph Banks, was a neighbour, and nearly of the same age. (Markham 1895, 82)

Rennell became a member of many learned societies and dining clubs, like so many of his circle. In 1781 he was elected Fellow of the Royal Society, and was a member of the select Royal Society Club until his death. In 1791 he received the Copley Medal of the Royal Society, and in 1825 was awarded the Gold Medal of the Royal Society of Literature (founded in 1820) as one of the first geographers of this or any other age or country, for his various and valuable illustrations arid improvements of ancient and modern geography (particularly by his maps and memoir of Hindostan and the neighbouring countries, by his memoir of the geography of the peninsula of Hindostan, by his memoir of the geography of Africa, and by his geographical system of Herodotus). (Brabrook 1897, 14)

COMPARATIVE GEOGRAPHY

Secondly, after Rennell's death in 1830, his daughter Jane Rodd edited his *A Treatise on the Comparative Geography of western Asia: accompanied with an atlas of maps* (1831), complete with an index but no obvious bibliography. The volume was sponsored by Lord Grenville, who helped to obtain support from King William IV (1765–1837), who was also patron of the newly formed Royal Geographical Society. Coincidentally, Lady Jane Rodd was advised by Lieutenant-Colonel Martin Leake FRS, late of the Royal Artillery and an influential figure in the African Association – who is also cited in the *Treatise* (1831) as an authority on Gaza – over any small difficulties that occurred. However, despite its thoroughness and accuracy, the text remains raw and unfinished and a difficult read; as Markham (1895, 121) wrote, it 'is the workshop, showing how the master worked with his geographical materials, and his method of building up the fair edifice which he left unfinished. It was a splendid conception, worthy of the great geographer.' It was compendious and exhaustive.

There were going to be 15 books in Rennell's comparative geography, each dedicated to a specific area (Asia Minor, Armenia, Arabian Desert, etc.). The 1831 volume contains five of these books. Concerned with the proper distribution of space rather than natural or political divisions, the first book, an overview of his model of comparative geography, contains a chapter on the Syrian Desert with lines of distance to various cities including Aleppo, Damascus, Siwah and Jerusalem. Rennell's methodology using these lines of distance was similar to the naval practice that gave rise to the Pontalan charts from the thirteenth century onwards.

The first part of the *Comparative Geography* covers the area between Siwah (then in Libya) and Persepolis in Persia (1600 miles) and between Zaritzin on the Volga and Upper Egypt and the head of the Persian Gulf (1350 miles). Book II deals with modern and ancient divisions of Asia Minor; the second chapter describes lines between Kaswin, Trabazond and the Caspian Sea; the third chapter connects Kaswin and Isfahan; the fourth chapter is on lines from the Sea of Marmara to Smyrna; and the fifth chapter on lines from Adrianople to the Danube, and so on. This compilation and subsequent correction of the ancient and modern geography of Western Asia was a very serious undertaking, requiring Rennell to balance one conflicting authority against another with amazing attention to detail.

Initially Rennell envisaged that the project would complement the compilations by the great French cartographer and geographer Jean Baptiste Bourguignon d'Anville that relied on ancient geographical sources. Like Rennell, d'Anville never visited the Middle East, and as a result, not surprisingly, Rennell found some of d'Anville's topography, especially in relation to the journeys by Alexander the Great and Darius, to be 'almost unintelligible' (1831, xxii) and quite contrary to historical accounts. For example, Rennell suggests that d'Anville must have used Ptolemy's map when he described the course of the Euphrates between Raqqah and Annah (1831, 50). In contrast, Carsten Niebuhr thought d'Anville's distances were pretty accurate along the Mediterranean coast (Rennell 1831, 64).

Geographers of the Enlightenment were concerned with scientific enquiry and precision. Rennell was fascinated with mathematical geography: identifying places and routes mentioned by travellers as 'collectors rather than interpreters of data' (Frantz 1932–3, cited in Damiani 1979, 10), a gap Rennell tried to fill. He not only studied the principal geographical writers of antiquity with the aid of translations, but also read the works of every minor author who travelled in the Middle East on which he could lay his hands. The acquisition of thorough scientific and human information was a heavy burden placed on any serious traveller. Rennell was concerned with accuracy and precise scrutiny of these travel sources. His meticulous approach was supported by myriad observations made by travellers in the region, who often carried with them a range of instruments including compasses, sextants, astrolabes and chronometers and provided useful scientific data on relative and specific locations. First, he took key, well-known locations and then used them to draw travel lines derived from as many reliable sources as possible between them and other places.

For the location of key points such as Jerusalem, Aleppo and Damascus he relied on many early sources including that by the Dutch mathematician and Orientalist, Jacob Golius (1596–1667). For the location of Aleppo and Damascus he also relied on Reverend Henry Maundrell's account in 1697 (1811), supported by information from a journal of 1687 by the French traveller and natural scientist, Jean Thévenot (1633–67). To pinpoint coastal towns, such as Tartus (called Tortosa by Rennell and the Crusaders), and central Syrian towns, such as Hama and Homs (1831, 64–6), Rennell used Thomas Shaw's travelogue (1738) because it described journeys in North Africa, Egypt, and the Middle East between 1731 and 1734. Some of the travelogues used by Rennell have been published by Douglas Carruthers, himself an explorer of the Syrian Desert, as *The Desert Route to India, Being the Journals of Four Travellers by the Great Desert Caravan Route between Aleppo and Basra, 1745-1751* (1929). But even Carruthers was unable to identify all Rennell's sources.

In addition to major classical sources and a wide range of European travelogues, Rennell found Arabic authorities – whom he termed 'Oriental geographers' – valuable in the study of routes and location of places, even though they were not always readily accessible to him. An authority that Rennell found reliable was Muhammad ibn Muhammad al-Idrisi (1100–62), who produced geographies for Sicily's Norman king, Roger II, and who travelled in North Africa, Turkey, and the Mediterranean. Other 'Oriental' sources he used included the ninth-century Persian astronomer al-Farghani (Alfraganus), the tenth-century Arab geographer Ibn Hawqal (AD 943–88) – author of *Kitab Surat al-ard* [*Depiction of the Earth*], which was based on al-Istakhri's *Kitab Masalik* [*Book of the Routes of the Provinces*] – and the twelfth-century explorer al-Idrisi. In turn, Ibn Hawqal and al-Idrisi were both used as authorities by Abu al-Fida (1273–1331), an Ayyubid prince of Hama (1831, xl). Furthermore, accounts by Pietro Della Valle (1650–63), the Italian traveller whose narrative voyages were written in letter form and divided into three parts (travels in Turkey, in Persia, and in India), and the German explorer, Adam Olearius (1603–71) – who was secretary to the ambassador sent by Frederick III, Duke of Holstein-Gottorp, to the Shah of Persia – were compared with those of Abu al-Fida (1831, 21). Rennell also gleaned information from the writings of Yaqut (1179–1229), author of a compilation of toponyms entitled *Mu'jam al-buldan*. Many of these Arabic authorities probably came from Rennell's study of d'Herbelot's *Bibliotheque orientale* (1776–83), and from discussions with Patrick Russell in London, who used them for his edition on Aleppo (1794). Such authorities included the twelfth-century Jewish adventurer Rabbi Benjamin of Tudela, the fourteenth-century Ibn Battuta's part-fact part-fantasy *rihlah*; and work of the seventeenth-century Arabic and Turkish geographer Hajy Khalifa (1831, 15).

For example, in trying to locate Rahabah on the Euphrates, Rennell quotes the Dutch philologist Albert Schultens' translation of Baha' al-din ibn Shaddad's life of Salah al-din, as well as al-Idrisi; Nasereddin (that is, Nasir al-Din al-Tusi), Timur's grandson *Uleg Beg* (1831, 50), who was a famous astronomer, and Gasparo *Balbi*, a Venetian jeweller, who travelled to India via Aleppo, Bir, the Euphrates and Baghdad in 1579. By comparing various accounts Rennell concludes that the Rahabah as described by Carmichael and al-Idrisi is not the same place as that recorded by the Frenchman G. A. Olivier in 1797 (Olivier 1801–07). Furthermore, Rennell compares distances given of the Euphrates, including an account by Isadore of Charax along the eastern banks, with that of M. Olivier, who travelled on the Arabian side (1831, 47), as well as journeys made by Edward Ives, a naval surgeon who went from Basra to Aleppo, via Diarbekr and Birejik and published *A Voyage from England to India* in 1773 (see Laughton 2004; Reddy 1968 3/2, 31–44).

On the section between Mesjid Ali and Basrah, Rennell relied on three main accounts: by Carmichael (Carruthers 1929); by an army officer and meteorologist Colonel James Capper, whose *Observations on the passage to India through Egypt* (1783) also contained his journal of the route through the Arabian Desert from Basra via Bagdad and Aleppo to Italy and England in March 1779 to February 1780; and by two explorers who crossed from Aleppo to Basra between 1770 and 1790 – John Griffiths MD (1805, 334), who was in the area in 1786, and Major John

Taylor (1794, 1799) of the Bombay Establishment, who was responsible for exploring communication possibilities between England and India (see Grant 1937 for further details). Other sources included those by Sir Robert Shirley (1599), who went from Aleppo to Baulus, near Tokat, via Bab in 1598, and Dr Leonhart Rauwolff (1693), who in 1674 navigated the Euphrates from Bir. This was about the time that some 'English gentlemen' who visited Palmyra in 1691 returned to Aleppo by way of Rasafah and Baulus. At the time Palmyra and much of the Syrian Desert was almost inaccessible as it was 'beyond the protection' of the Sultan of Turkey (Grant 1937, 102).

Alongside factual accounts of the relict features of the ancient worlds, Rennell gave particular credibility to a range of seventeenth- and eighteenth-century travellers in the Syrian Desert, especially the factual accounts by Maundrell, Carsten Niebuhr (1792), Richard Pococke (1743–5) and consul Alexander Drummond (1754). Rennell greatly respected the accuracy of Maundrell's account, with its careful measurements and plans of major sites such as Baalbek, and that of the Friesian mathematician and mapmaker, Carsten Niebuhr (1733–1815), using his account, for example, to determine the lines between Hillah on the Euphrates to Brusa. Many of Niebuhr's maps and papers about Asia Minor were destroyed in a fire about 1797, but Rennell proudly claimed to own a copy of the map of Niebuhr's route, struck off from the copper before the fire (Leake 1824, xvii). Rennell admired the accuracy of Drummond's account and that of Pococke, considering that the quality of Pococke's observations made him one of the most important Near Eastern travellers. This was despite the fact Pococke did not always visit the places he claimed he had seen, and much of Drummond's account was written by the novelist Tobias Smollett. Even minor authorities, such as Mr C. R. Vaughan – who seemed to have travelled 'very fast' across the Syrian Desert to Persia in 1804 – were meticulously studied for his identification of precise locations along and across travel lines. The accuracy of William G. Browne's lines across Asia Minor, as well as of his descriptions of Siwah from his notes lodged in the East India Company library and later published in 1820 by Robert Walpole, particularly impressed Rennell; Browne was murdered in Persia in 1813 and buried at Miyana, next to the French traveller and natural scientist, Jean Thévenot (1633–67).

Many papers consulted by Rennell were collected by Orme for his *A History of the Military Transactions of the British Nation in Indostan from 1745* (1763–78), which has been described by Macaulay (1841 3, 85) as

> inferior to no English historian in style and power of painting [but] is minute even to tediousness In one volume he allots on an average a closely printed quarto page to the events of every forty eight hours The consequence is that his narrative though one of the most authentic and one of the most finely written in our language has never been very popular and is now scarcely ever read.

Ironically, several items in Orme's collection were actually papers that Rennell had originally lent to Orme to help the latter compile his history. They include transcriptions of several manuscripts written by travellers across the Syrian Desert that had been lent to Rennell by Patrick Russell MD (d.1805) or his brother Claud, including those by William Beawes (quoted in Fortenberry and Manley 2009, 51–2) and by Carmichael. Rennell felt exasperated when Orme refused to return these materials. 'It is a provoking circumstance,' he wrote, 'that the Historian O-e keeps up all the Geographical materials in order to extract such particulars only as serve the purpose of illustrating his History: and probably I may either lose my eyesight, or drop into the grave before he has done with them.' (*Survey of India 1945*, 22).

EARLIER PARTS OF THE COMPARATIVE PROJECT

Rennell published two or three parts of his lifelong comparative geographies project before his death in 1830, including a life of Herodotus (1800, revised 1830). It was in the second volume of his 'Geography of Herodotus' that he laid the foundations of his interest in travellers in Egypt and North Africa and, coincidently, in the rate of travel by camels.

Other parts of his grand project included a topography of the plain of Troy (1814), in which he discussed sources as diverse as Xenophon and Anabasis and tried to rectify the faulty topography presented in the *Tableau de la plaine de Troye* by Jean-Baptiste Le Chevalier. In his identification of Troy, Rennell was criticised by Charles Maclaren (1822), the editor of *The Scotsman*, who argued that Rennell based his identification of its location on Homer, which was actually based on misinterpretations of Homer by Strabo.

Another section of Rennell's comparative geography project was published as *Illustrations (chiefly geographical,) of the history of the expedition of Cyrus, from Sardis to Babylonia* (1816), in which he discussed the location of Babylon using work on Cyrus by the Greek historian, Xenophon, who was sent into exile, served with Greek mercenaries in Kurdistan, Armenia and Asia Minor, and wrote *Anabasis Kyrou* [*The retreat/expedition of Cyrus*], a personal account of his adventures. Xenophon's descriptions were compared by Rennell with archaeological reports, classical (Strabo, Pliny, Polybius, and others) and Arabic sources (al-Idrisi. Abu al-Fida, Ibn Hawqal, Ibn Battuta and others). Three maps of the routes of Cyrus, and Xenophon, compiled by Rennell in 1809, 1815, and 1816, are now held by the Society of Antiquaries of London (shelfmark B 29e Case).

One of the sources Rennell used in his work on Cyrus in determining the position of the source of Murad river and the location of various villages was Morier's travelogue (1812, 74, 210–13, 311). A British diplomat who grew up in

Figure 2. The Museum at East India House. Charles Knight (ed.) (1851).

Smyrna (Izmir), where his father was a merchant of the Levant Company, James Justinian Morier was famous for his delightful *Hajji Baba of Ispahan* novels (1823 onwards), set at the time of the Qajar dynasty in Iran, as Johnson describes (1998). Although Rennell also drew some of Morier's maps, he did not have time to incorporate into his *Comparative Geography* (1831) the material about Armenia and Persia he gleaned from Morier's travelogue. Coincidently, this was a volume that was edited, in part, by Sir Robert Harry Inglis 2nd Bart (1786–1855), a prominent arch-Tory MP and active evangelist, and son of Rennell's close friend, Sir Hugh Inglis. As a complement, in the introduction to his second travelogue (1818, ix), Morier acknowledges the kind advice and ready help he received from Major Rennell and also cites Rennell's works on Herodotus (1818, 235, 266) and Babylon (1818, 207).

In 1797, Hugh Inglis had written to the Bombay Presidency ordering the Resident at Bassorah to procure some Babylonian bricks from Hillah. The outcome was the arrival of the 'Babylonian Stone', one of the earliest acquisitions of the India Museum, which is now in the British Museum, where it is known as the 'East India House Inscription' (BM registration number 1938,0520.1). Sir Harford Jones-Brydges, a fluent Persian speaker and not a man to be crossed, was the Company Resident at Baghdad from 1798 to 1806, having previously served in Basra (1783–94), and it was he who obtained the stone for East India House in 1801. Whilst he is mentioned in Rennell (1831), it was only after Rennell's death that Jones-Brydges published several accounts of his experiences in Persia (1833, 1834).

The Babylonian stone was rapidly translated by Dr Joseph Hager – *A Dissertation*

Figure 3. Bassorah from the Euphrates. Captain Robert Mignan (1829).

on the newly discovered Babylonian inscriptions (1801) – and continued to stimulate great interest in Babylon. Claudius James Rich, the former Resident of the Honourable East India Company at Baghdad, published *The Ruins of Babylon* (1815). With all the interest in Babylon, in 1816 Rennell compiled *Remarks on the topography of Ancient Babylon* (1816, 1817). This was subsequently criticised by Rich in his *Second Memoir on Babylon* (1818), firmly disagreeing with Rennell's findings, which were largely based on Rennell's interpretation of accounts by an Italian nobleman and traveller, Pietro Della Valle: 'Diffident as I am in opposing my ideas to such an authority, I feel myself called upon to state that I cannot coincide with Major Rennell, either in his interpretation of the ancient writers, or in his deductions from the actual appearance of the ruins.' (1818, 140) Rich pointed out fiercely that little more could be learned without excavation. His widow Mary Rich continued to publish on this topic after her husband's death in *Narrative of a journey to the site of Babylon in 1811* (1839), criticising the accuracy of some of Rennell's archaeological data. She also continued to publish Rich's travelogues such as *Narrative of a residence in Koordistan* (1836) and a *Journey from Bussora to Bushire, Shirauz, Persepolis, &c.* (1839). (For more on the Rich family travels see Oliphant 2009, 41–52.)

In his *Travels in Mesopotamia* (1827), James Silk Buckingham, who had recovered from sunstroke in Rich's house in August 1816 (1827, 496), firmly endorsed his host's findings (1827, 418–19):

> On gaining the summit of this large mass, we had the first sight of the Euphrates, flowing majestically along through verdant banks, and its serpentine course apparently losing itself in the palm-groves of Hillah, whose mosques and minarets we could just perceive, about five miles to the southward of us. We had from hence, too, a very commanding view of the ruins around us, which seemed to correspond so perfectly with the Plan accompanying Mr. Rich's Memoir as to leave nothing to be added to that interesting document.

Whilst acknowledging Rennell as an 'authority ... deservedly so high with regard to ancient geography and local positions', Buckingham supports Rich's authority over that of Della Valle (1827, 423).

There were other smaller papers published as part of Rennell's project, including two articles in *Archaeologia*, one 'On the voyage, and place of shipwreck, of St. Paul, AD 62' (1827 21, 92–106), read before the Society of Antiquaries in 1824 (Markham 1895, 183–7), concluding that this took place in Malta rather than in the Adriatic; and another 'Concerning the identity of the architectural remains at Jerash: and whether they are those of Gerasa, or of Pella' (1827 21, 138–47), an interest stimulated by Dr Seetzan's discovery in 1806, John Lewis Burckhardt's descriptions (1822), and by careful surveys by Captains C. L. Irby and J. Mangles (1823). Rennell identified Jerash with the ancient Gerasa, a conclusion which is now universally accepted (Markham 1895, 180–2).

CAMELS

In the days before satellite imaging and sophisticated cartographical methods, accurate distances between remote locations were hard to assess. Rennell was particularly fascinated by the rate of travel by camels in the desert (1831, xlix–li). He had previously presented a paper to the Royal Society on 17 March 1791 entitled 'On the rate of travelling as performed by camels: and its application, as a scale, to the purposes of geography', later published in their *Philosophical Transactions*, and this is the fourth reason why Rennell deserves to be included in this book.

Rennell provided detailed comparisons of a range of units of distance, including the 'Arabian mile' and 'Persian farsangs', as well as assessments on the rate of travel of camels as reported by a wide range of travellers who crossed the Syrian Desert. Based on careful study of travel accounts, Rennell recorded that 'they were about 19 hours in going from this latter [northern] route to Aleppo; and for which 2 ⅔ per hour (by horse) may be allowed' (1831, 35). Other sources included the third-century *Antonini Itinerarium*, a register of the stations and distances along the various roads of the Roman empire, which gives distances in Roman miles (Roman paces were not everywhere the same, and conversion to modern units is imprecise, but one Roman mile equals 1479 metres); and the *Theodosian Table*, a source also used by Burckhardt (1822). Rennell also cites many other authorities who crossed the Syrian Desert, including a 'Journal of the Travellers, in 1702', which was communicated to Rennell by Mr Claud Russell, brother to Dr Patrick Russell (1831, 281–2). Local authority was provided from maps by Ibrahim Effendi, a Hungarian who introduced printing and copperplate engraving to Constantinople.

In particular, Rennell found the account of distances and rates of travel by Carmichael in 1765–6 (whose account was also used by Niebuhr) to be very accurate, and gave him credit 'for taking incredible pains' (1831, 24). Setting off from Aleppo, Carmichael made a credible survey of the 520 miles to Basra. His caravan included 50 horses, 30 mules, and 1200 camels, 600 of them laden with merchandise then valued at £300,000. A troublesome character, Carmichael was finally dismissed from service in the East India Company in Bombay and was obliged to take the desert route via Syria from London to India in order to settle his affairs. He subsequently returned to India and worked for various local Indian rulers. but died impoverished in Surat.

AFRICAN ASSOCIATION

A fifth reason for including Rennell in this volume was his involvement in publishing largely posthumous accounts by, and providing maps for, explorers in Egypt and North Africa who had been sponsored by the African Association. The Association for Promoting the Discovery of the Interior Parts of Africa (the African Association) was essentially a dining club founded at a dinner held by the Saturday's Club (from 1799 the African Club) at St Paul's Tavern off Pall Mall, London in 1788 (Sinclair 1901 1(1), 145–9; Sattin 2003), by an influential group including William Wilberforce and the banker Thomas Coutts. It was led by Sir Joseph Banks, 'the great panjandrum of British science in the period' (Wagstaff 2003), and by the Quaker abolitionist, Henry Beaufoy. By 1791 the Association had 95 members, and sponsored a series of important one-man explorations until 1831.

Rennell was elected as an honorary member in 1792 as the Association's surveyor and cartographer, but also helped to publish various expedition journals. Indeed, many of the dignitaries of the African Association edited and published these explorers' posthumous accounts. For a while after Banks's death in 1820, Rennell attempted to fill the gap as its president; but later the presidency was held by John Barrow, Secretary to the Admiralty (Association for Promoting the Discovery of the Interior Parts of Africa 1964).

Amongst his other projects for the African Association, Russell annotated and published (1802) a journal of an expedition to Siwah and across North Africa by the German explorer Frederich Konrad Hornemann, after the explorer disappeared in 1800. However, a French translation of the English work, made by order of the First Consuls and augmented with notes and a memoir on the Egyptian oases by L. Langlès, was published in Paris in 1803 and is now considered the more valuable version. Rennell provided maps and appendices for the English edition, including 'Geographical illustrations of Mr. Horneman's route; and additions to the general

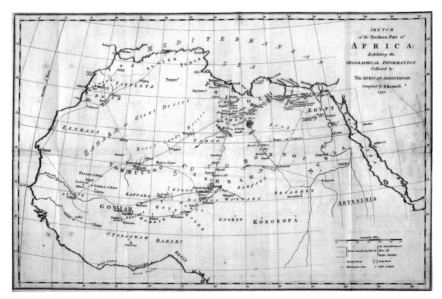

Figure 4. J. Rennell (1790) Sketch of the Northern part of Africa: exhibiting the geographical information collected by the African Association.

geography of Africa' (Hornemann 1802, 121–88), alongside an introduction by Sir William Young, who wrote (1802, v):

> the writer would refer, as a special instance, to the elucidations of Major Rennell: … to that most accurate and acute philosopher and geographer, the details have afforded matter of enquiry and deduction of the highest import to science. By analysis, and a comparative view of accounts given of journeys and places, in reference to the plans of D'Anville, and other geographers; to modern travels; to ancient expeditions; to descriptions of ancient writers; and above all, to those of the father of history, Herodotus; Major Rennell hath corrected the map of Africa, with a learning and sagacity which *hath converted conjecture into knowledge.;* and on experience of those who have explored parts of that great continent, given confidence to each future traveller who may visit its remotest regions.

Rennell was also interested in other aspects of Egypt and North Africa through the African Association, and was involved in many of their other projects. The African Association published the communications of, briefly, Mr Ledyard and, chiefly, Mr Lucas, on their journeys in northern Africa, these travels being compiled from papers lodged with the Association (1790). Simon Lucas spoke fluent Arabic, having spent some time in Morocco. He arrived in Tripoli in October 1788, and planned to travel across the Libyan Desert, but he was deserted by his guides during tribal wars and abandoned his expedition. Rennell provided a relevant map, which was published several times between 1790 and 1804 as a

'Sketch of the Northern part of Africa: exhibiting the geographical information collected by the African Association', with manuscript additions and a manuscript memoir. In 1798 he also provided 'A map, shewing the progress of discovery & improvement, in the geography of North Africa' for the Appendix to Mungo Park's *Travels* (1799); it was later revised for Hornemann's travels. In 1790, Rennell provided another map for the travels of the American John Ledyard (1751–89). Ledyard arrived in Cairo in August 1788 but fell ill, and died from an overdose of medication in Cairo.

In 1827 the Raleigh Club, a dining club designed entirely for travellers, was created (Markham 1895, 195) and included Rennell and many of his friends. The navy was very strongly represented, as was the army, and it continued to flourish until 1854, when it was renamed the Geographical Club, and was in close association with the Royal Geographical Society. At a meeting of the Raleigh Club in May 1830, called by Sir John Barrow, the Secretary of the Admiralty, it was unanimously decided that a Geographical Society was needed, with its aims being

> to print geographical information for its members, to accumulate a library and a collection of maps and charts, to procure instruments for the information and instruction of travellers, to prepare instructions for explorers and give them pecuniary assistance, to correspond with similar Societies and with geographers in all parts of the world, and to open communication with all philosophical and literary Societies with which geography is connected. (Fitzroy and Raper 1854, 24, 328–58)

In 1831 the African Association was absorbed by the Royal Geographical Society, which, during its formation in 1830, had planned to offer the presidency to Rennell, then aged 88. However, on 29 March 1830, before it was finally constituted, Rennell died. He was interred in the centre of the nave of Westminster Abbey; the explorer David Livingstone (1813–73) was later buried near him.

CONCLUSIONS

There were many more reasons why Major James Rennell deserves a place in a book on Near Eastern travel, not least his network of friends and his family heritage. His grandson, the poet and diplomat James Rennell Rodd (1858–1941), First Baron Rennell of Rodd, helped negotiate a treaty in 1897 with Emperor Menelik II of Ethiopia, served in Egypt and was ambassador to Italy from 1908 to 1919. His great-grandson, Francis Rennell Rodd (1895–1978), 2nd Baron Rennell, was a great friend of the Egyptian explorer Ahmed Hassanein Bey and travelled in the Sahara (Starkey 2010). Either he or his father wrote a biographical note about James Rennell (Rennell Rodd 1930, 289–99). After his death the substantial Rennell collection of over 450 books, including 22 items from the direct distance subject to error. Mr. Eyles Irwin, who was so eminently successful in estimating the distances across the desert, (having calculated that from Aleppo to Bagdad at 493 British miles by the road, and it actually appears to be about 480), computes the road distance at 106 B. miles. Mr. Drummond, whose distances are often over-rated, allows 110 ; and Mr. Ives 102. So that Mr. Irwin's is an *exact mean* between the others. Allowing the error of Mr. Irwin's calculation on the desert, which is scarcely 2¾ in 100, the result will be 79 G. miles direct ; differing from M. Niebuhr's only one mile. The mean 78½, laid off from Aleppo, to the parallel of 35° 31′, places Latikeah in longitude 35° 46′, or 1° 23′ west of Aleppo.

In Rúm-Ili.	Hours.	G. Miles.
Mr. Bell, Ismael to Burgos	97	2·6
M. Sturmer	60	2·6
Captain Hayes	20	2·6
In Asia Minor, &c.		
Mr. Browne, Brusa to Iconium, through Kutahiah, &c. . . . . }	81½	2·62
———— Smyrna to Libad	51	2·39
Mr. Sullivan, Nicomedia to Amasia	129	2·2
Dr. Howel, ditto	123	2·31
Mr. Drummond, Syria, (horseback)	179½	2·45
Mr. Maundrell, ditto (on foot)	44	2·38
Mr. Ives, Bagdad to Mosul	104½	2·12
Dr. Howel, Hillah to Mosul	115	2·31
Major Leake, Isnik to Iconium	93	2·165
Caravans, in Asia Minor.		
Dr. Seetzen, Smyrna to Iconium	121½	2·24
Mr. Browne, Aintab to Nicomedia	230¼	1·826

Figure 5. A: An example of intertextuality employed by J. Rennell (1831); B: An example of statistics provided by J. Rennell (1831).

library of James Rennell, were left to the Royal Geographical Society (Johnson 1978 148/1, 38–42).

What is critical to any study of early travellers in the Middle East is Rennell's exhaustive, if exhausting, use of sources written by travellers in the Middle East at a time when

> [t]he characteristic travel book of the 18th century is a ponderous quarto or folio, handsomely printed, often beautifully illustrated, and conveying much leisurely information concerning monuments, customs and costumes … as a rule, these productions have about them little of the personal spirit, little of the lighter literary touch which gives vitality to travel books. (Kirkpatrick 1907 14, 246)

Rennell's cross-fertilisation of travel narratives written by travellers from different backgrounds and training was stimulating, even though the sources of the comparative geographies are a challenge to any modern scholar to disentangle. There is no time here to list all the authorities cited in Rennell's many works, and in the *Comparative Geography* (1831) in particular, but they were amazingly comprehensive. Unfortunately there is no bibliography provided in Rennell (1831), which makes identification of some of the sources difficult. Mohammad Ali Hachicho has compiled a useful and thorough list of travellers in the Levant during the eighteenth century in his excellent essay (Hachicho 1964 NS 9, 1–206), but not all Rennell's sources are listed there.

Rennell's work emphasises the close connections between geography and history. Critically, history

> was not possible without location, and what the map provided was a perspective on a bounded space which married well with History's need for 'abstracted

particulars' – where the fact, or the location on the map, could be taken as a representation of itself, as capable of comparison, and as information which itself encapsulated a story. (Rennell 1910, 137–8)

The wide range of travel narratives of the Middle East cited as sources by Rennell reflects the complexity of his approach and his extraordinary attention to the detail. Subsequent to Rennell's work, Markham despaired (1895, 208):

Until this connection is impressed upon the rising generation of travellers, and is present in their minds, we shall continue to be deluged with rubbish in the form of books of travels, and we shall look in vain for the charm which is felt in reading the works of travellers who were also scholars and observers.

BIBLIOGRAPHY

Arrian (1809) *The Voyage of Nearchus, and the Periplus of the Erythrean Sea*, trs. from the Greek by Dr William Vincent. Oxford, At the University Press, for the author; and sold by Messrs. Cadell and Davies in the Strand, London.

Association for Promoting the Discovery of the Interior Parts of Africa (1790) [Journeys of Mr. Lédyard and Mr Lucas in Africa] *Proceedings of the Association for promoting the discovery of the interior parts of Africa* 1, 1–238.

Association for Promoting the Discovery of the Interior Parts of Africa (1804) *Voyages de MM. Lédyard et Lucas en Afrique*. Paris, Chez Xhrouet, Déterville.

Association for Promoting the Discovery of the Interior Parts of Africa (1964) *Records of the African Association: 1788-1831*, ed. R. Hallett for the Royal Geographical Society. London & New York, T. Nelson.

Brabrook, E. W. (1897) *The Royal Society of Literature of the United Kingdom. A brief account of the origin and progress.* London, Asher and Co.

Buckingham, J. S. (1827) *Travels in Mesopotamia*. London, Henry Colburn.

Burckhardt, J. L. (1819).*Travels in Nubia*. London, John Murray.

Burckhardt, J. L. (1822) *Travels in Syria and the Holy Land*. London, John Murray.

Burney, F. & Barrett, C. (1854) *Diary and Letters of Madame D'Arblay*. London, Henry Colburn.

Capper, J. (1783) *Observations on the passage to India, through Egypt, and across the great desert; with occasional remarks on the adjacent countries, and also sketches of the different route.* London, printed for W. Faden, J. Robson and R. Sewell.

Carruthers, A. D. M. (1929) *The Desert Route to India: being the journals of four travellers by the great desert caravan route between Aleppo and Basra, 1745-1751*. London, printed for the Hakluyt Society.

D'Anville, J. B. B. (1779) *l'Euphrate et Le Tigre*, 5 vols with a map. Paris, s.n.

D'Herbelot de Molainville, B. (1776–83) *Bibliotheque orientale ou dictionnaire universel.* Maastricht, Jean Edme Dufour & Philippe Roux 1776; The Hague, 4 vols 1777–1799; Paris, 6 vols. 1781–1783.

Damiani, A. (1979) *Enlightened Observers: British Travellers to the Near East, 1715-1850*. Beirut, American University of Beirut.

de Thévenot, Jean (1687) *The Travels of Monsieur de Thévenot into the Levant. In three...parts: I. Turkey. II. Persia. III. The East-Indies*, trans. A. Lovell. London, printed by H. Clark, for H. Faithorne, J. Adamson, C. Skegnes, and T. Newborough repr. Farnborough, Gregg (1971).

Della Valle, P. (1650–63) *Viaggi di Pietro della Valle, il pellegrino: con minuto ragguaglio di tutte le cose notabili osseruate in essi; discritti da lui medesimo in 54. lettere familiari... mandate in Napoli all'erudito... Mario Schipano, diuisi in tre parti, cioè la Turchia, la Persia, e l'India.* Rome, appresso Vitale Mascardi.

Drummond, A. (1754) *Travels through different cities of Germany, Italy, Greece, and several parts of Asia as far as the banks of the Euphrates: in a series of letters. Containing, an account of what is most remarkable in their present state, as well as in their monuments of antiquity.* London, printed by W. Strahan for the author.

Fitzroy, R. and H. Raper, H. eds (1854) Hints to travellers, *Journal of the Royal Geographical Society* 24, 328–58.

Fortenberry, D. and Manley, D. eds (2009) *Saddling the Dogs; Journeys through Egypt and the Near East.* Oxford, Oxbow Books.

Frantz, R. W. (1934) *The English Traveller and the Movement of Ideas, 1660-1732.* Lincoln, University of Nebraska Press.

Gladwin, F. (1780) *A compendious vocabulary English and Persian.* Bengal, printed by Charles Wilkins.

Grant, C. P. (1937) *The Syrian Desert: caravans, travel and exploration.* London, A & C Black.

Griffiths, J. (1805) *Travels in Europe, Asia Minor and Arabia.* Edinburgh, Peter Hill, printed by John Brown.

Hachicho, M. A. (1964) English Travel Books about the Arab Near East in the Eighteenth Century, *Die Welt des Islams* NS 9, 1–206.

Hager, J. (1801) *A Dissertation on the newly discovered Babylonian inscriptions.* London, Wilks & Taylor, printers, for A. Tilloch, sold by Messrs. Richardsons.

Hornemann, F. (1802) *The Journal of Frederick Horneman's* [sic] *travels: from Cairo to Mourzouk, the capital of the kingdom of Fezzan, in Africa. In the years 1797-8.* London, printed by W. Bulmer and Co. Cleveland-Row, St. James's; for G. and W. Nicol, booksellees [sic] to His Majesty, Pall-Mall, repr. London, Darf, 1985.

Irby, Hon. C. L. and Mangles, J. (1823) *Travels in Egypt and Nubia, Syria, and Asia Minor, during the years 1817 and 1818.* London, privately printed.

Johnson, A. M. (1978) The Rennell collection, *The Geographical Journal* 148/1, 38–42.

Johnston, H. M. (1998) *Ottoman and Persian Odysseys: James Morier, creator of Hajji Baba of Ispahan, and his brothers.* London, I. B. Tauris.

Jones-Brydges, H. (1833) *The Dynasty of the Kajars, Translated from the Original Persian Manuscript.* London, John Bohn.

Jones-Brydges, H. (1834) *An Account of the Transactions of His Majesty's Mission to the Court of Persia in the years 1807-11.* London, printed for James Bohn.

Kirkpatrick, F. A. (1907) The Literature of Travel, 1700–1900, in A. W. Ward and A. R. Waller (eds), *The Cambridge History of English Literature: the nineteenth century III* 14, 7–246. Cambridge, Cambridge University Press.

Knight. C. ed. (1851) *London.* London, Henry G. Bohn.

Laughton, J. K. and Ives, E. (*d.*1786), rev. E. Baigent, *Oxford Dictionary of National Biography.* Oxford, Oxford University Press [accessed 17 Nov 2004, http://www.oxforddnb.com/view/article/14499].

Le Chevalier, J.-B. (1791) *Description of the plain of Troy: with a map of that region, delineated from an actual survey.* Edinburgh, printed for T. Cadell.

Leake, W. M. (1824) *Journal of a tour in Asia Minor, with comparative remarks on the ancient and modern geography of that country.* London, John Murray.

Macaulay, Baron T. B. (1841) *Critical and Miscellaneous Essays.* London, Carey & Hart.

Maclaren, C. (1822) *A Dissertation on the topography of the Plain of Troy, including an examination of the opinions of Demetrius, Chevalier, Dr. Clarke, and Major Rennell.* Edinburgh, printed for A. Constable.

Marco Polo (1818) *The Travels of Marco Polo* translated from the Italian, with notes by W. Marsden. London, Longman.

Markham, C. R. (1895) *Major James Rennel* [sic] *and the Rise of Modern English Geography.* London, Cassell & Co.; repr. BiblioBazaar, LLC, 2009.

Marsden, W. (1783) *The history of Sumatra.* London, printed for the author.

Maundrell, H. (1811) *A Journey from Aleppo to Jerusalem at Easter, AD 1697,* in J. Pinkerton (ed.), *A General Collection of the best and most interesting voyages and travels in all parts of the world: many of which are now first translated into English; digested on a new plan.* London, Longman, Hurst, Rees, and Orme.

Mignan, R. (1829) *From Travels in Chaldaea, including a journey from Bussorah to Bagdad, Hillah, and Babylon, performed on foot in 1827.* London, Henry Colburn and Richard Bentley.

Morier, J. J. (1812) *A Journey through Persia, Armenia, and Asia Minor, to Constantinople, in the years 1808 and 1809: in which is included, some account of the proceedings of His Majesty's mission, under Sir Harford Jones, Bart. K. C. to the court of the King of Persia... and three maps;... two drawn by Mr Morier and Major Rennell.* London, printed for Longman, Hurst, Rees, Orme, and Brown.

Morier, J. J. (1818) *A second journey through Persia, Armenia, and Asia Minor, to Constantinople, between the years 1810 and 1816: with a journal of the voyage by the Brazils and Bombay to the Persian Gulf.* London, Longman Hurst Rees Orme and Brown.

Niebuhr, C. (1792) *Travels through Arabia and Other Countries in the East,* trans. Robert Heron 2 vols. Edinburgh, printed for R. Morison and Son.

Oliphant, M. (2009) From Baghdad to Constantinople on Horseback: a journey by Claudius and Mary Rich, October-December 1813, in D. Fortenberry and D. Manley (eds), *Saddling the Dogs,* Oxford, Oxbow.

Olivier, G. A. (1801–07) *Voyage dans l'Empire Othoman, l'Égypte et la Perse. Fait par ordre du Gouvernement, pendant les six premieres annees de la Republique. 3 vols, with Atlas.* Paris, H. Agasse.

Orme, R. (1763) *A History of the military transactions of the British nation in Indostan: from the year 1745: to which is prefixed A dissertation on the establishments made by Mahomedan conquerors in Indostan.* London, printed for John Nourse.

Park, M. (1799, repr. 2003) *Travels in the Interior Districts of Africa: performed under the direction and patronage of the African Association, in the years 1795, 1796, and 1797.* London, Eland Publishing.

Pococke, R. (1743–5) *Description of the East: containing Observations on Egypt, Palestine, Syria, Cyprus, Canclia, the Greek Islands of the Archipelago, Asia Minor, Thrace, Greece, Italy and Germany, 2 vols in 3.* London, printed for author by W. Bowyer; and sold by J. and P. Knapton *et al.*

Pryme, J. T. and Byne, A. (1879) *Memorials of the Thackeray family.* London, Spottiswoode and Co., for private distribution.

Ray, J. (1693) *Collection of Curious Travels & Voyages in two tomes the first containing Dr. Leonhart Rauwolff's Itinerary into the eastern countries..., the second taking in many parts of Greece, Asia Minor, Egypt, Arabia Felix and Patraea, Ethiopia, the Red-Sea.* London, printed for S. Smith and B. Walford.

Reddy, D. V. S. (1968) Medical observations of Dr Edward Ives, a naval surgeon (1754–1757), *Indian Journal of the History of Medicine* 13/2, 31–44.

Rennell, J. (1790) Sketch of the Northern part of Africa: exhibiting the geographical information collected by the African Association [London], J. Rennell. map. *Proceedings of the Association for promoting the discovery of the interior parts of Africa,* 1, 211.

Rennell, J. (1790[-1792]) Sketch of the Northern part of Africa, exhibiting the geographical information collected by the African Association: compiled by J. Rennell. 1790. [With ms. additions and a ms. Memoir.] London, J. Rennell; another edition Paris, 1804.

Rennell, J. (1791) On the rate of travelling as performed by camels; and its application, as a scale, to the purposes of geography, *Philosophical Transactions of the Royal Society (London)* 81 , 129–45.

Rennell, J. (1798) The route of Mr. Mungo Park from Pisania on the River Gambia, to Silla on the River Joliba or Niger; with his return by the southern route to Pisania, compiled from Mr. Park's observations, notes & sketches, by J. Rennell (J. Walker sculpt.). London, J. Rennell.

Rennell, J. (1814) *Observations on the topography of the plain of Troy: and on the principal objects within, and around it described, or alluded to, in the Iliad, shewing that the system of M. de Chevalier.* London, G. & W. Nicol.

Rennell, J. (1816) *Illustrations (chiefly geographical,) of the history of the expedition of Cyrus, from Sardis to Babylonia; ... Explained by three maps.* London, printed by W. Bulmer and Co. and sold by G. and W. Nicol.

Rennell, J. (1816) *Remarks on the topography of Ancient Babylon: suggested by the recent observations and discoveries of C. J. Rich ... From the Archæologia.* London, T. Bensley.

Rennell, J. (1817) On the topography of ancient Babylon: suggested by the recent observations and discoveries of Claudius James Rich, Esq. *Archaeologia* 18, 243–62.

Rennell, J. (1827) Concerning the identity of the architectural remains at Jerash: and whether they are those of Gerasa, or of Pella. *Archaeologia* 21, 138–47.

Rennell, J. (1827) On the voyage, and place of shipwreck, of St. Paul, AD 62. *Archaeologia* 21, 92–106.

Rennell, J. (1830) *The Geographical System of Herodotus examined and explained,* 2 vols. London, C. J. G. & F. Rivington.

Rennell J. (1831) *A Treatise on the comparative geography of western Asia: accompanied with an atlas of maps* 2 vols. London, printed for C. J. G. & F. Rivington.

Rennell, J. (1910) *The Journals of Major James Rennell, first Surveyor-General of India, written for the information of the Governor of Bengal during his surveys of the Ganges and Brahmaputra rivers, 1764-1767,* ed. T. H. D. LaTouche. Calcutta, The Asiatic Society.

Rennell, J.(1800) *The Geographical System of Herodotus examined and explained,* 2 vols. London, printed by W. Bulmer and Co. for the author, and sold by G. and W. Nicol.

Rennell Rodd, (F.?) (1930) Major James Rennell. Born 3 December 1742. Died 20 March 1830, *The Geographical Journal* 75/4, 289–99.

Rich, C. J. (1815) *The Ruins of Babylon.* London, Longman, Hurst, Rees, Orme, and Brown.

Rich, C. J. (1818) *Second memoir on Babylon, containing an inquiry into the correspondence between the ancient descriptions of Babylon and the remains still visible. Suggested by the "Remarks" of Major Rennell in the Archæologia.* London, Longman, Hurst, Rees, Orme, and Brown.

Rich, C. J. (1836) *Narrative of a residence in Koordistan, and on the site of ancient Nineveh: with journal of a voyage down the Tigris to Bagdad and an account of a visit to Shirauz and Persepolis.* London, J. Duncan.

Rich, C. J. (1839) *Narrative of a journey to the site of Babylon in 1811, now first published; Memoir on the ruins, with engravings from the original sketches by the author; Remarks on the topography of Babylon, by Major Rennell, in reference to the memoir; Second memoir of the ruins, in reference to Major Rennell's remarks; with a Narrative of a journey to Persepolis, now first printed, with hitherto unpublished cuneiform inscriptions copied at Persepolis* edited by his widow. London, Duncan and Malcolm.

Richardson, J. (1810) *A Dictionary, Persian, Arabic, and English: with a dissertation on the languages, literature, and manners of Eastern nations... with numerous additions and improvements by Charles Wilkins.* London, printed by William Bulmer & Co. for F. and C. Rivington.

Ritchie, A. T. (1913) *From the Porch.* London, Smith, Elder & Co; repr. BiblioBazaar, LLC, 2009.

Russell, A. (1756) *The Natural History of Aleppo.* London, printed for the bookseller, Andrew Millar; 1794. Second edition, revised, enlarged and illustrated with notes by [his half-brother] P[atrick] Russell, 2 vols. London, printed for G. G. and J. Robinson.

Sattin, A. (2003) *The Gates of Africa: Death, Discovery and the Search for Timbuktu.* London, Harper Collins.

Schultens, A. (trans) (1732, 1755) *Vita et res gestæ sultani, Almalichi Alnasiri, Salah al-Dini,* Leiden, apud Joannem Le Mair.

Shaw, T. (1738), *Travel or Observations Relating to Several Parts of Barbary and the Levant.* Oxford, printed at the Theatre.

Shirley, A. and R. B. (1599) *A True Report of Sir A. Shierlies Journey overland to Venice ... to Antioch, Aleppo, and Babilon.* London, R. B., for I. I.

Sinclair, W. (1901) The African Association of 1788, *Journal of the Royal African Society* 1/1, 145–49.

Starkey, J. (2010) Into the desert: reality or unreality? Francis Rennell Rodd and Ahmed Hassanein Bey. Paper presented at the WOCMES Conference, Barcelona.

Survey of India (1954) *Historical Records of the Survey of India*, collected and compiled by R. H. Phillimore. Vol. 3, 1815 to 1830. Dehra Dun, Survey of India..

Taylor, J. (1794) *Considerations on the practicability and advantages of a more speedy communication between Great Britain and her Possessions in India – With an Outline of a Plan for the more Ready Conveyance of Intelligence overland by the way of Suez.* London, printed by C. Macrae.

Taylor, J. (1799) *Travels from England to India in the year 1789, by way of the Tyrol, Venice, Scandaroon, Aleppo, and over the Great Desert to Bussora; with instructions for Travellers; and an account of the expence of travelling.* 2 vols. London, printed by S. Low; for J. Carpenter; and Murray and Highly.

Vetch, R. H. (2004) Thackeray, Frederick Rennell (1775–1860), rev. Roger T. Stearn, *Oxford Dictionary of National Biography*. Oxford, Oxford University Press.

Wagstaff, M. (2003) Review of A. Sattin (2003) *The Gates of Africa: Death, Discovery and the Search for Timbuktu.* London, HarperCollins. *ASTENE Bulletin* 17.

Walpole, R., and Browne, W. G. (1820) *Travels in various countries of the East:being a continuation of Memoirs relating to European and Asiatic Turkey, &c.* London, Longman, Hurst, Rees, Orme, and Brown.

Wilkins, C. trans. (1785) *The Bhagavat-Geeta: or dialogues of Krishna and Arjoon, in eighteen lectures; with notes / translated from the original. in the Sanscrit, or ancient language of the Brahmans.* London, printed for C. Nourse.

A Journey Through the Holy Land, 1820

Deborah Manley

Many of the young men who went to the Near East in the early nineteenth century seem to have had the urge to travel for no very apparent reason. Rather like today's gap year travellers, there was perhaps in this wanderlust a desire to break away from family life and grow up, before settling down to real life and even an occupation – although, as we know, 'gentlemen' did not 'work' – but some of these young men had truly historic adventures. For example, the young clergymen Barnard Hanbury and George Waddington went to Egypt in 1823, sailed up the Nile to Nubia, and became involved in Egypt's war in Dongola. This adventure cannot have been mere chance; one wonders why they were there just then, in an almost official position.

What gave these young men this urge to travel? Reverend Robert Master (1794–1867) was a clergyman who rose to become Archdeacon of Manchester. Towards the end of his Eastern journey he explained his reasons for travel to the Orthodox Archbishop of Smyrna (whom he met through Mr Wilkinson, the Levant Company chaplain with whom he was staying). The Archbishop, Master wrote, was 'a tall, fine-looking man with an expressive countenance and a long grey beard flowing over his breast, and always accompanied by half a dozen people'. The Archbishop expressed himself as much surprised that one so young as Master – then about 23 – could be an English clergyman, and asked him his reasons for travelling. Master's reply gives us at least the arguments one such traveller used.

> It was for the sake of improvement and of taking home personal impressions of foreign lands, and all they had to teach, and of visiting and examining the localities renowned in ancient history and venerable from their still existing temples and monuments, since these places had been the study of his youth, and he had read the various authors who described them in the zenith of their celebrity and glory.

The Archbishop was even more satisfied with Master's answer when he learned that the young man had toured Palestine and the several places rendered sacred by the birth, the life, the sufferings and the death of Our Lord.

One's choice of companions for such journeys was, of course, very important. In 1818 Master had set out with Sir Archibald Edmonstone, who published an account of their discoveries, based in part upon Master's journal, and one Henry Hoghton. Clearly Master and Edmonstone got on easily; the younger man, Hoghton, seems to have been the odd one out, and was left out of some of their activities. Master was clearly saddened when, in July 1819, after nine months of travel, Edmonstone left the other two at Smyrna, according to a previous arrangement. Master wrote that they had travelled together 'most agreeably, without having once had a desire to separate ... a thing', which, he recognised, 'is not often the case with travellers'.

Unusually, in this unpublished journal we have a personal view of one traveller by another. The Victorians might have thought it 'bad form' to publish comments on a friend. But here, privately, Master wrote of Edmonstone affectionately: 'His high spirits and his anxiety to leave no subject of interest unexamined made him a most charming companion.' He also had a 'a store of amusing stories to enliven the tedium of the evenings'. Those long evenings and nights must sometimes have hung somewhat heavily upon travellers.

The trio's original plan was a traditional one: to sail up the Nile, return north again and then continue on to the Holy Land – nothing unusual in that. But when there were already on the Nile, they decided – seemingly almost casually, though Edmonstone claimed this journey was already in his thoughts – to try to become the first Europeans within memory to reach the oases of the Western desert, Dakla and El Kharga, and to beat the real Egyptian adventurers, men like Colonel Drovetti and Giovanni Belzoni, at their game. The resulting book, *Journey to two of the oases of Upper Egypt*, published in 1822, is important in the annals of Egyptian travel.

That book tells of their travels and discoveries in Egypt, but after Egypt Robert Master continued to maintain his journal, which was copied in a fair hand by his son years later. The approximately 300-page manuscript of that copy is now in the Manuscript Library of the British Library (add.MS 51313). The manuscript's earlier pages are illustrated with Master's on-the-spot sketches of people and places. It is entitled *Journal of a Tour in Egypt, Palestine and Greece in the years 1818, 1819.* Master, Edmonstone and Henry Hoghton returned to the Nile from the desert in March 1819. On a sortie up the Nile to the island of Philae, they encountered British Consul General Henry Salt, who with William Bankes and other travellers had been on the Nile for some weeks, but was about to return to Cairo.

Then, despite reports of plague in the north, the trio set off for Cairo. By the time they arrived, Salt was already back in the consular house and took them under his wing, showing them his drawings of Upper Egypt and Nubia, which he proposed to offer his travelling companion, Mr William Bankes. One of these Master thought a painting of great beauty – a chariot and horses from the tombs at Thebes, the trappings of which he compared to 'those in use at the present time' (Master, 226).

Master was interested in the impact of the plague, but found contradictory opinions about its source and effect. He noted optimistically that 'cases of recovery are not infrequent' and the regularity of its appearance in February and March meant that Franks 'almost to a day knew when to close their doors against others'. I judge that his study of plague was not without personal interest – and legitimate fear. 'I was told', he reported, 'that in Cairo in about 1803, 30,000 of Cairo's 400,000 inhabitants were carried off within three days.'

Master reported what he heard – probably mainly from Salt – of Pasha Mehemet Ali, and of the Wahabees, who the previous year had been 'dislodged from their Arabic strongholds'. Whoever was telling of the Wahabees, they painted a frightening picture: 'very savage, almost naked, murdering and drinking the blood of their prisoners' (Master, 227).

The trio did not stay long in Cairo; having sorted out cash and hired camels, they set off for Jaffa on Friday, 15 April 1819. They left their 'mummies and other curiosities' to be forwarded on to 'Mr Briggs the banker's house in London'. They found their dromedaries, well padded with carpets, comfortable enough if one frequently changed position. Master gives far more detail of this part of the journey than most. They grew nervous as they rode out beyond Mehemet Ali's territory and, as often happened, they were joined by other travellers, looking for protection in numbers. About sunset on 26 April they reached the safety of Gaza. One can almost hear Master's nervous sigh of relief (Master, 232).

In Gaza they took up their quarters at the Dagana or khan. There they found gathered in the courtyard 'all kinds of merchandise brought by passing caravans'. Above was a higher floor with small chambers, which they found 'sufficiently filthy'. They chose the best room and settled down for the night, paying the bill the next day with a case of gunpowder. Master was much taken with Gaza: 'embosomed in gardens, the hills around it clothed in wood'. He had seen nothing like it since leaving Italy (Master, 232). Now Master had come to a familiar place, where he must have felt he knew the land and certainly knew its history. At the entrance to the city, he was reminded of Judges XVI.3, how Samson carried away the gates, for in 1819 they had been more recently removed. 1 Kings IX 17 reminded him of the rebuilding of Gaza by Solomon after its destruction by the king of Egypt.

Until they arrived in the Holy Land proper, Master had not referred to biblical links, but from now on his bible knowledge came to the fore. He followed the route and the sites as recorded in the Bible, and believed this rather than the information provided by their guides. For instance, at Ascalon they found a fortress and fruit trees 'but not a single dwelling', in accordance with the prophecy of Zacharia: 'Ascalon shall not be inhabited.' As an ordained minister, Master is a very different type of traveller from the gentlemen travellers – observant as ever, but linking what he sees to the Old and New Testaments' learning and beliefs, with marginal notes of chapter and verse.

In Jaffa on 25 April they were stopped at the city gates, but were, gratifyingly, immediately admitted 'on announcing our nationality', and proceeded to the house of the English consul. The somewhat eccentric Dr Damiani – described by other travellers – was absent, but his son welcomed them in.

Jaffa impressed Master with its 'commanding appearance', and he was pleased to report that one of the bastions of the fortified wall had been built by Sir Sydney Smith during the Napoleonic troubles. But the town was 'dirty in the extreme'; the harbour – much used by pilgrims – he deemed 'the worst in the Mediterranean'. Yet it was here, he knew, that Solomon ordered the materials for the Temple to be brought, and Pliny tells us that Jaffa is older than the Deluge. There is even a tradition that Noah himself lived here and built the Ark here, and the city is named after his son Japhet.

More recently, Master recalled the terrible massacre of the 'Turks' – and some Christians – a slaughter believed to have been committed by Napoleon. Although this account was even then being denied by many, Damiani's son, a boy of ten at the time, remembered the tale and that his father had 'made notes of everything and transmitted his notes to the Consul at Aleppo'.

At their next stop, Ramla, the trio stayed comfortably with the Franciscans, in one of three convents, the other convents here and elsewhere being Greek and Armenian Orthodox. On departing they gave the padre superior three dollars and he offered to give them a mass apiece in return.

The town and the roads around were crowded with pilgrims returning from Jerusalem at this Easter season. They passed an assorted company of at least a thousand on their way. It was a 'motley and ludicrous assemblage', Master recorded, of all ages, riding horses, camels and asses, the camel panniers 'filled to repletion – a leg protruded from one, an arm from another, and there a head resting uneasily upon the edge of a hamper'. Some wore turbans, some hats with 'brims as wide as umbrellas'. Many carried palm branches, twigs from the Jordan and rosaries from Bethlehem (Master, 229). The road was narrow and Master complained that this great multitude 'caused some hindrance' to their progress. He wondered that, with this traffic coming every year since the Crusades, no improvement had been made to this road. A further problem he reported were the Arab robbers, 'who have their haunts in caverns, once sepulchres or perhaps dwelling places of the ancient Phillistines'. But soon they were approaching Jerusalem. The valley corresponded exactly to the description given in the book of Samuel (1 Samuel VII, 3), as the setting for David's victory over the Philistine giant, Goliath, and they had even crossed the very brook from which David had selected 'the five smooth stones' (Master, 234). They rode up a rugged road and gained the summit, which overlooked the Holy City, resembling, Master thought 'a baronial stronghold'.

It was late by the time they reached the city walls, and the gates were locked. It took two hours to gain entry and it was midnight by the time they reached the Franciscan convent where they were to stay. In the morning, 1 May, they were pleased as they looked around the comfortable room they were to share, with a separate kitchen and a special cook to prepare their meals at their own convenience. One of the fathers was always available, 'anticipating and supplying our wants'. They particularly studied the names of past travellers carved on the door of their room. They recognised the names of Thomas Shaw, there in 1722, and Edward Daniel Clarke, who had stayed nearly twenty years before them. They had either read Clarke's book or actually had it with them, and often compared his knowledge with their own. It may be that they knew him at Cambridge, where Clarke was Professor of Mineralogy and from 1817 University Librarian.

The next day they met the padre superior, a Maltese priest who was in failing health. Most of the other priests were Spanish and, despite what Clarke's descriptions had led them to expect, none were corpulent, and 'none of them filled out their habits'.

Master asked about the religious groups in Jerusalem. There were said to be about 5000 Christians, of whom 700 were Catholics. 'The Jews,' they were told, 'are numerous, occupying a special part of the city.' The monks were very critical of 'the extortion and greed' of the Turkish rulers. Master was impressed by the care offered to any indigent Catholics in the convent's care. 'They had ever at hand a friend in need – a physician, education and training for their children, and care for their souls.' Master, a non-Catholic, wished for 'the long-continued prosperity of the Convent'.

The men visited the Governor of Jerusalem and received passports for their onward journey. From the Governor's window they looked out on the beautiful mosque of Omar, built on part of the site of Solomon's temple in AD 637. They would have known from their meetings in Egypt that this mosque had been entered in the previous year both by William Bankes and his dragoman, Giovanni Finati, and by Sarah, Giovanni Belzoni's wife. When the journal was being written up Master knew of Dr Richardson's friendship with the Governor and his official entry to the mosque.

Then, as today, visits to the sites of Jerusalem were steeped in biblical knowledge. Here was the scene of the 'scourging and mocking of Jesus'. Here the stairs he descended from Pilate's palace had once been, but they had long since been transported to Rome. The church of St Anne was said to have been built on her home – where Mary had been born – but had been desecrated and was now used as a stable. To a believer, some of these stories must have been painful. In the evening they attended a special service at the Church of the Holy Sepulchre on the anniversary of the discovery of the True Cross.

A few days later they set out on horseback to see 'some remarkable spots outside the walls': Bathsheba's pool, the valley of Gethsemane, and the cave where the apostles hid before they fled. The three men looked out over the vale, watered by the pool of Solomon, 'which smiles with fertility'. Nearby, Judas died by his own hand (Master, 284). Master sketched the sepulchre, to which they were guided, and described it in detail. The city wall ran along the ridge of the opposite hill. At a corner stood the short end of a column, upon which, it was said, Mohammed would take his seat on the Day of Judgement while all the world would be assembled in the valley beneath (Master, 238).

They ascended the Mount of Olives and visited Bethany, where Lazarus' tomb was to be visited. Nearby, a stone marked the spot where Martha met the risen Jesus. At the summit of the mount, 'the Turks have a mosque, part of which, they understood, was once a church in honour of the Ascension. A small chapel there was still reserved for the Latins, built, they believed, where Jesus last stood on Earth – and where the print of his foot is seen on the rock.' St Luke, Master knew, had beatified a quite different place. From nearby high ground there was a magnificent view of Jerusalem, and looking the other way they saw the Dead Sea and the distant ranges of Arabia Petraea.

There were many, many more sites to visit: where the Apostles' creed was composed; the olive grove through which Our Saviour passed, although Master had read his Josephus and knew better; a stone marking a spot where Mary 'let fall her girdle at her assumption'. It was all there to be explained, but the trio had seen enough and retreated back to the city, pausing for further sites on the way. At last they reached their comfortable room in their convent home after five, having been tourists for ten long hours.

The next day they set out for Bethlehem, stopping by a well where the star appeared to the Magi. On arrival they settled comfortably into the Franciscan convent, before visiting the grotto of the Nativity and seeing the manger in which Our Lord was laid. The sites at Bethlehem were shared with the Greeks and Armenians, and Master wrote of a split about access – of which the Turks took advantage and the Latins, who were reporting the tale to them, lost out. They spent further days in the area around Jerusalem, but were, it seems, beginning to grow weary of tourism. Master and Edmonstone spent 7 May sketching and examining the various spots likely to have been the actual site of the crucifixion and the resurrection. They concluded that these could not be indicated with precision, and decided that Clarke had got it wrong.

On the Sunday, they spent the day at the Church of the Holy Sepulchre. They were sprinkled with rose water, and saw some beads being blessed, thinking 'the prayer being uttered with the utmost rapidity and irreverence' (Master, 246). As they heard more and more links to both Old and New Testaments, Master recorded with increasing doubt. Their sense of history and of the timescale became increasingly overpowering. They betook themselves too to the synagogue, and they went to the Schismatic Syrian church, built, it was said, over St Mark's dwelling, and passed on to the Armenian convent, which they greatly admired. They were shown, stored below the altar, the stone which closed the mouth of the holy sepulchre. 'This,' Master reported coolly, 'the worthy fathers stole many years ago' (Master, 244).

The next day, 10 May, they set off for the Dead Sea, a journey recorded with the same attention. They pitched their tent in Jericho that night, and the next day went with a guard of ten armed men for the Jordan. There they indulged themselves in a bath – as did the soldiers, who washed themselves and their horses and swam for a considerable time. Master knew that on Easter Monday some 2000 pilgrims and the governor and his guard of 700 men came here. 'This devotion', Master had been told (just possibly by Sarah Belzoni, who had been there herself, and whom Master had met on the Nile with her husband), 'carries them all into the water, without distinction of sex.'

They carried away twigs from the wooded bank, 'which they deem to be charms and endowed with occult virtues'. They found their day at the Dead Sea fascinating, although they do not seem to have entered the waters and floated upon them. They returned to Jerusalem on 12 May and set out on the next leg of their journey on Saturday, 15 May. They departed through the Damascus Gate and an hour later turned to take their last look at the Holy City.

The places along the way were still closely linked to their knowledge of the Bible and early Christianity. They saw the church built by the Empress Helena to revere the place where Mary sought her lost child, and Bethel, 'where Jacob was favoured with the vision of the Angelic ladder'. The road was rocky, the land hardly cultivated, although it showed signs of past cultivation.

For the next leg, for the first time on their long journey through Egypt and Palestine, the trio found difficulty in travelling. They had trouble getting accommodation – that night the only space on offer was in the mosque, with 'the local people persisting in coming in and intruding upon our privacy, notwithstanding repeated requests that they would retire and leave us in repose' (Master, 248). However, the men were sometimes made welcome, and continued with their daily round of ancient sites.

A slightly cynical – even jocular – air began to creep into Master's journal;

one feels that they were becoming sated by the supposed links of this land to history. Even the Sea of Galilee disappointed. It being the bathing season, 'such numbers of people thronged the baths, that we had no opportunity of properly examining them'. From there – no accommodation being offered – they travelled through the night, an activity which would certainly have been very risky at other times.

At last the potential comforts of Acre lay ahead, but the town gate was closed and they were told 'some Jewish travellers had lately conveyed the plague into the town' (Master, 254). However, they were later admitted into the very welcome Franciscan convent near the Frank khan. Here one senses that the men relaxed after this uncomfortable stretch of their journey, and Master contemplated the people whom they had passed. 'The population of all the country through which we have lately passed', he wrote, 'is Arab.' They were, he explained, 'descended from the conquerors of that race, with some intermixture of the native races'. 'They are', he continued, 'wilder than their Egyptian brethren.' This he explained by the weakness of the government, in contrast with Egypt, where Mehemet Ali had then ruled for well over a decade, 'and of the mountainous nature of the district' (Master, 255). The people, he reported, 'are always armed, and continually engaged in skirmishes with each other'. Their usual costume Master described as a loose cloak, striped white and blue, or white and brown, worn over a white shirt. The Bedouin, he noted, were darker complexioned than other Arabs and their horses were particularly celebrated, for their beauty and performance. The Bedouin lived primarily upon the borders of the desert as far as the Jordan and the Dead Sea. 'They are', Master noted with admiration, 'quite independent, their hand against every man.' They wore, instead of the turbans of other Arabs, a loosely tied headkerchief.

The party never received 'any molestation' from the Bedouin, unlike later travellers, but the other peoples of the area suffered from them, suddenly discovering them encamped on their cultivated land or even taking possession of their strongholds. Recently, they were told, the Pacha of Damascus, returning from Jerusalem with a considerable treasury, had been attacked and plundered and, when the Pacha retaliated, the Bedouin gave better than they got (Master, 356).

Master reported with interest that, in battle, the women accompanied the men, encouraging them by their warlike songs and assisting them with slings 'in the use of which they excel'. He had heard that the Bedouin of Barbary go into battle accompanied by the Sheikh's daughter mounted on a camel and beating on a tambourine, 'her hand being the prize of him who first brings her the head of an enemy. Master and others usually referred to Muslims as 'Turk' or 'the Turks' – who were, of course, also the rulers of the Ottoman empire. He saw two sides of them – often harsh rulers, and careless with the land and with the buildings, both ancient and modern, on the one side, but 'remarkable for both hospitality and charity, as enjoined by the Koran'. 'A Turkish beggar', he noted, 'is unknown.' The peasants were effectively slaves, he noted, being a conquered people, 'but the word means little more than subject'. The peasants were not, he said, feudal property, as in Russia.

They were disappointed by Acre – they had seen so much that was larger, better preserved, more historic, that they were almost bound to be disappointed. Master was more excited by a visit to Mount Carmel, with its single but optimistic monk.

They were now to sail northwards, and Master 'lamented much' at not being able to visit Tyre and Damascus and Baalbec and the magnificent cedars of Lebanon, but time pressed and the captain of a boat in the harbour was on the point of leaving. On Thursday, 28 May 1819, they 'bade adieu to Palestine, embarking at sunset, and being towed out of the harbour but making little further progress in consequence of unfavourable winds'.

After very variable winds, both lacking and too strong, occasional times ashore when Master copied inscriptions wherever he could, and a visit of several days in Smyrna – from whence Edmonstone left them for Constantinople – on Saturday, 10 July Master and Hoghton started early one morning with an easterly wind, rounded Cape Sounion, and ran along the coast of Attica, commenting that, despite everything that must have been poured into this land for centuries, 'the nature of the land is so sterile that industry expends its strength in vain'. But, he continued: 'Bye and by we sighted the long wished for Acropolis of Athens upon a rocky eminence, towering over the adjacent plains and crowned with the superb remains of its ancient edifices.' (Master, 265) All they had learned during years of an early nineteenth century classical education must have welled up in them.

They were inspired too by the thought of exchanging their seafaring life for the comforts of civilisation. In a small inlet at Salamis they bathed – 'no small luxury' after sleeping in their clothes 'with nothing but hard boards to lie upon'. Master went for a walk and found himself looking down on 'the very spot where that famous engagement between the Greek fleet and that of Persia took place'. The wind changed, and near dawn they entered the harbour of Piraeus. Within two hours, riding through olive groves, they entered Athens.

The town itself seemed to consist of 'mean houses, standing in narrow, dirty and unpaved streets – with an almost entire lack of activity and life'. Athens seemed to have nothing on Smyrna, which they had greatly enjoyed. But the place grew on Master as did the people, and they soon found a comfortable house and an excellent servant and I leave them here before they eventually headed for home, and the life that lay ahead.

BIBLIOGRAPHY

Manuscript

Master, R. *Journal of a Tour in Egypt, Palestine and Greece in the years 1818, 1819.* Manuscript Library of the British Library (add.MS 51313).

Publications

Belzoni, G. (1820 *Narrative of the operations and recent discoveries ... in Egypt.* London, John Murray.

Clarke, E. D. (1814) Travels in Various Countries of Europe, Asia and Africa – Part the Second, Greece, Egypt and the Holy Land, Sections I and II, London: T. Cadell & W Davies.

Edmonstone, A. (1822) *Journey to two of the oases of Upper Egypt.* London, John Murray.

Death and Resurrection:
the Renans in Syria (1860–61)

Geoffrey Nash

An early American biographer summed up Ernest Renan's archaeological expedition to the Near East in the barest outline:

> October 18, 1860, Renan left Paris for Syria, where he was engaged in excavations and travels for nearly one year. After a trip to Jerusalem he wrote his *Life of Jesus* at Ghazir. On September 24, 1861, his sister Henriette died at Amschit, while he too was suffering from fever. He reached Paris October 24. (Mott 1921, 2007)

We are perhaps accustomed to viewing a journey as the raw materials of a piece of travel literature, be it a volume worked up from letters home, a notebook or diary, or simply a work elicited directly from memory. Renan's official report, *Mission de Phénicie*, is precisely that – it encompasses the public side of his journey, and is of interest for its articulation of his report on the ancient Phoenician remains of Lebanon. The private record is to be found in the letters he wrote to his friend Berthelot, and in his subsequent memoir, *Ma Sœur Henriette*. But the *Life of Jesus*, with which this paper is primarily concerned, is a work in which travel, biography and mission intersect. In fact this might be seen as the proper epitome of Renan's journey: through visiting the scenes of his life and 'living in imagination the life of Jesus' (Wardman 1964, 73), he was able to write Jesus' biography with his sister at his side. Her death and his return to Paris to take up the chair in Hebrew at the Collège de France led Renan to experience both a personal death and also a personal resurrection.

While the loss of Henriette brought him face to face for the first time with the possibility that life had no meaning, the book would establish his fame/ notoriety, unlocking the themes of his maturity: the backward look at humanity's mytho-religious past; the view forward to a Europe without faith mired in secular, racial hatred; and beyond to our own time's clash over the sites of 'civilization's birthplace and the presumed heart of the modern malaise' (Lee 1996, 188). This last strand is articulated in the book by the passages that bitterly attack the Muslim presence in the sites which Renan had so recently reconnoitred in Lebanon and Palestine.

On arrival in Lebanon, Renan seems to derive a frisson from finding evidences of the struggle of dead cultures buried in the earth. That he came prepared for and immediately settled into a quasi-messianic role is evinced by a letter he wrote to Berthelot within a month of arriving in the Near East:

> My mission is getting on perfectly; we are going to make excavations on a large scale, in company with the army. The naval authorities are also very obliging, and have, with great kindness, placed a steamer at my disposal. It was desired to make short sojourns during the winter, and to set up establishments all along the coast; the pre-text for this has been found. Fuad is very well. Fuad and Ismail [his two helpers] are men; the rest of the Turks are stupid or ignoble. This country is lost to Turkey without hope of redemption. But what will become of it? This is one of the most puzzling problems in the world when it is examined at close range. *The strange role that one plays here is alone worth the voyage* (my italics). You cannot imagine how many things of the past are explained when you have once seen this country. (Renan 1904, 148)

The last sentence is chilling. Digging up the past could so easily mean, especially for Renan in suave but combative mood, resurrecting old feuds and perhaps in the process inventing new ones.

Renan clearly enjoyed the escort of French soldiers and the imperial cachet they lent his expedition. In the context of 1860, France had sent a military force to protect the Maronites from further massacre by the Druse. As Frederick Bliss, surveying nineteenth-century archaeological exploration of the Holy Land, engagingly phrases it: 'when so desired, the French soldiers, by Imperial command, exchanged their swords for spades' (Bliss 1906, 242). The presence of the soldiers also made a political statement which is reinforced in Renan's letters. In these he did not attempt to hide both his sympathies for the Maronites and his contempt for the Turks (in his parlance the 'Metuwalis') as well as Greek Christians, both Orthodox and Catholic. Ann Neville sees in the scientific commission Napoleon I took with him to Egypt in 1798 the 'obvious precedent' to Renan's expedition, and while she admits Renan's operated on a much less grandiose scale (Neville 2002, 231, 232), it might be observed that they are alike in at least one particular: both had peremptory, fateful endings, occasioned in Napoleon's case by defeat at the hands of Britain, and in Renan's by personal tragedy. As for Renan's competence as the leader of an expedition whose purpose was to investigate the 'archaeological evidence for Phoenician culture', which Neville points out was disputed at the time, she notes he was aided on the ground by a capable team of collaborators, none of whom, however, possessed specific archaeological expertise, though she characterises his work as 'meticulous' and 'scientific' (Neville 2002, 230). Bliss dismissed the Frenchman's adoption of *a priori* rationalisation in favour of empiricism, taking him to task for failing to carry out a systematic excavation at Byblos: 'We admire Renan's learning and ingenuity, but we cannot help feeling that these are set to work on slight and insufficient data. Had he supplemented his free use of learning with a freer use of the spade, the world might have been richer in actual knowledge.' Not for the last time a reviewer of Renan's career charged him with theoretical indulgence at the expense of fact: 'To exhaust the search for data before constructing theories should be the prime law of the scientific excavator.' (Bliss 1906, 250)

Renan's archaeological project centred, from north to south, on 'four campaigns': Ruad (Aradus), Jbail (Byblos), Saida and Sour (Sidon, and Tyre) (Bliss 1906, 244). From late November 1860 to early February of the following year, he was at Jbail excavating the site of Byblos and staying at nearby Amshit. The site encouraged him to believe that its ancient Semitic inhabitants the Giblites were near ancestors of the Hebrews, one of their words for God *Adonai* being the same as the Hebrew. Even at this stage in history he read into the inscriptions a struggle between Semitic and Hellenic civilisation: Adonai had conquered Adonis. The struggle had continued into the Middle Ages, with Christians painstakingly smashing the remains of temple inscriptions in a systematic idolatry. The country had never recuperated but had 'been killed by Christianity; it was already in ruins when the Moslems arrived; the Christians finished it' (Renan 1904, 154–5).

In the spring the focus switched south to Sour and the ancient city of Tyre. 'This country is ... admirable,' he writes to Hippolyte Taine in March, 'Lebanon has a great charm, *un reste du parfum* which it has had since the time of Jesus. I am already on Biblical territory. I see from my terrace Sarepta, Hermon, Carmel, the mountains of the tribe of Dan.' He could not help remembering how the beauty, the profane organisation and wise government of Tyre had revolted the prophets as 'true Israelites, representatives of the ancient theocratic spirit in its brutal simplicity' (Renan 1947–61, x.307). In the April and May the Renans would spend a total of 34 days in which they visited 'all the places associated with the career of Christ', returning north in the heat of summer, tired out 'by the hardships and fatigues of exploration' (Mott, 211). Brother and sister retreated first to Amshit in the hills above Jbail, where Renan continued his archaeological work, and thence to Ghazir in the mountains above Beirut, where he started writing up his notes to produce by mid-September a first draft of his *Life of Jesus*. The work that had brought Renan and his sister so closely together after his apparent neglect of her for archaeology, was 'one reason, perhaps the most important, why he had accepted the invitation to the Middle East' (Wardman 1964, 74). But Henriette died just as Renan had reached the point in the narrative that dealt with the Last Supper.

Variously seen as a self-portrait, an exercise in nature-worship, and a piece of fiction, *The Life of Jesus* would simultaneously embody a romantic evocation of the landscape of Galilee not uninfluenced by Renan's native Brittany, and a condemnation of the Semitic principle he saw embodied in theocratic Judaism and (for him) its Islamic heir. (See Moxnes, H. (2003) for a detailed and perceptive reading that sets Renan's journey alongside his *Life of Jesus* and Orientalism.) The book's hostility to Judaism fed into the nineteenth century's anti-Semitic rhetoric and cannot be absolved of connection to the degradation all Europe had a hand in, in the century to come. It ran together with its author's researches into the Phoenician remains of Lebanon and sympathy for the Maronites, some of whom would later embrace an imagined non-Arab Phoenician ancestry (see Salibi, K. 1988, Kaufman, A. 2004). *The Life of Jesus* pits Islam against Christendom, fixing the work firmly within the later twentieth and early twenty-first century's clash of civilisations discourse matrix. In addition, it wafted a fresh air across Victorian religious orthodoxy, Catholic and Protestant alike, delivering what the secularist might celebrate as a blow in favour of spiritual freedom, encapsulated by St Beuve's encomium: 'You have won for us the right of discussion on this matter, hitherto forbidden to all.' (Mott 1921, 239)

The representations of Galilee, still so fresh in his mind, are integral to Renan's declared aim, as he writes to Berthelot on 12 September 1861, of giving his account 'an organic continuity which is entirely lacking in the gospels'. 'This idea of a living organism,' he states in the introduction to *The Life of Jesus*, 'we have not hesitated to take as our personal guide in the general arrangement of the narrative' (Renan 1935, 25). Renan's organically conceived narrative of the gospel accounts is clearly mediated by his personal experience of the Holy Land, and structured in turn by his reading of the gospels. But his response to the landscape of the holy places, unlike that of other Victorian travellers, notably Harriet Martineau, is not frozen by the biblical text. The connections he makes with his own times are shaped by his philological learning, by his obsession with the Semitic and Aryan principles he saw working through history, and a personal, nineteenth-century facility of being 'still capable of recalling [his] Christian origins with sympathy and nostalgia, even as [he] was persuaded to renounce them as childish fantasies' (Lee 1996, 188). As Schweitzer put it: 'He offered readers a Jesus who was alive, whom he, with his artistic imagination, had met under the blue heaven of Galilee, and whose lineaments his inspired pen had seized.' (1954, 181) Renan was also a rational historian, who brought to his subject a capacity for re-working the first-century materials with an agnostic nineteenth-century European mind not unlike FitzGerald's reproducing Omar Khayyam, bent on giving a mature order to the 'childish' disorder of his oriental sources.

Galilee is turned into a paradise for natural man, rich in all those aspects lacking in the Judean desert which had, he argued, helped form the stark judgemental, apocalyptic monotheism of orthodox Judaism. In contrast (and the contrast was axiomatic to his view of Jesus) the freer, softer moral teaching of Jesus accorded far better with the Galilean landscape which Renan describes in language similar to that found in a famous passage from Josephus:

> The whole area is excellent for crops and cattle and rich in forests of all kinds, so that by its adaptability it invites even those least inclined to work on the land ... It is thickly studied with towns, and thanks to the natural abundance the innumerable villages are so densely populated that the smallest has more than 15,000 inhabitants. (Wilson 1993, 124)

Renan contrasts this with the hard conditions of life in Europe:

> In our societies, established upon the very rigorous idea of property, the position of the poor is horrible; they have literally no place under the sun. There are no flowers, no grass, no shade except for him who possesses the earth. In the East these are gifts of God which belong to no one. The proprietor has but a slender privilege; nature is the patrimony of all. (Renan 1935, 101)

'This terrestrial paradise' encouraged a pietism based on direct charismatic connection between the ordinary people of Galilee and the inspired teacher, rather than the forbidding legalism of the Pharisees. Renan's portrait does not in fact contradict the Jewish Jesus produced by relatively recent scholarship. In his celebrated study, *Jesus the Jew*, Geza Vermes assigns Jesus to the category of spiritual healers, exorcists, miracles workers and prophets known among the people as *Hasidim*, or pure ones. He accentuates his Galilean provinciality and locates him within what Flusser terms an '"inevitable tension" between charismatic and institutional Judaism' (Vermes 1973, 80). This is not far distant from Renan's democratic man of the people, although he is, as Schweitzer noted, evasive about the miracles. Indeed, for the rigorous Teutonic mind of Schweitzer, Renan's idyllic tableau of Jesus and his disciples in Galilee is too easily populated with *belles creatures* in the form of beautiful women who vie with one another for *le plaisir* of listening to Jesus and tending to the needs of the *charmant, suave et douce* young rabbi. It was not just 'the lyrical and sentimental, the artificial, the subjective in the worst sense of the word' that angered the German theologian and missionary in Renan's portrait, it was its poor aesthetic quality – 'Christian art in the worst sense of the term – the art of the wax image' (Schweitzer 1954, 185, 181, 182).

While intelligent readers have noticed the nature-worship especially evident in the earlier chapters dealing with Jesus' first Galilee period before he left for Jerusalem, today we cannot fail to apprehend Renan's emphasis of personal revulsion for the nineteenth-century Muslim settlements that (he believes) intentionally came to overlay the sites identified with Christ. Whilst still in Lebanon he wrote to Berthelot: 'It is impossible to have any idea of the devastation of this country. All that has been said falls short of the truth. *It is the paradise of God devastated by the frightful Tartar demon* [i.e. the Ottoman Turk. My italics]. Happily all the world now seems agreed to drive him out.' (Renan 1904, 149)

As for Jesus' beloved haunts around Lake Tiberius – Magdala, Dalmanutha, Capernaum, Bethsaida and Chorazin – these had been replaced by a collection of villages, one of which bears a name corrupted from the original Magdala. 'The repulsive village of Medjdel has no doubt preserved the name and the place of the little town which gave to Jesus his most faithful female friend.' Overall, however, it seemed that 'in topography, as well as in history, a profound design has wished to conceal the traces of the great founder'. 'It is,' Renan continues, 'Islamism, especially the Mussulman reaction against the Crusades, which has withered as with a blast of death the district preferred by Jesus.' Going further, he arraigns the Christianity of the Crusaders along with Islam, its 'rival' in 'fanaticism', for both coveting Galilee, which 'as the price of its glory, has been changed to a desert' (Renan 1935, 89, 90, 91). Today, some may even see added irony in the fact that the Muslim presence that Renan clearly saw as a simulacrum for the Phariseeism against which his Jesus railed, is, as a result of a further twist in the clash of cultures, in the early twenty-first century in process of being erased by a Jewish state.

In Jerusalem and its vicinity, however, Renan appears not to have been disappointed:

> Here, assuredly, are Bethphage, Bethany and the Mount of Olives, the places beloved of Jesus. Gethsemane is not far from this little region; according to some monks, it is near a group of very old olive-trees. Yonder is Bethsaida, Siloam and its fountain. Golgotha was not far from where they now place it. This road cut in the rock, and descending from Galilee, has certainly borne the footprints of Jesus, and is certainly the place where he received from these poor bands of Galileans that triumph at the hands of the poor which cost him his life. (Renan 1904, 179)

Nevertheless, having placed his subject in a paradisiacal Galilean countryside, Renan disrupts the idyll by taking him south to Judea, where he is confronted by the ugly monotheism of official Judaism. First of all in the desert terrain in which John the Baptist had featured, but even more so in the city, Jesus' message of love comes up against the distortions of legalistic fanaticism. Above all in Jerusalem, by now 'no longer a Jew' but 'in the highest degree revolutionary' and would-be 'destroyer of Judaism', Jesus is confronted by 'laws of an intolerant theocracy' then embodied in the temple, afterwards to be refurbished in the *haram al-aqdas*: 'the last place in the world where revolution could prosper. Imagine an innovator going in our days to preach overthrow of Islamism in the mosque of Omar!' (Renan 1935, 123, 124, 181, 195)

The struggle between Jesus, the hard-line Pharisee and his Muslim descendants – Islam was a 'sort of resurrection of Judaism' (Renan 1935, 121) – which he projected on to the landscape of Palestine, lodged in his mind as a battle between what he considered to be the two polar principles of civilisation: Hellenism and Semitism. In *Life of Jesus* Renan lays the foundation for the later works in his *Origins of Christianity* series which, as Lee points out, 'show him initially disposed to annex Christianity to his own Aryan culture and values and to denounce or belittle the contribution of Old Testament Israel' (Lee 1996, 215). For Lee the oscillation between the Hebraic and Hellene aspects of his intellectual and spiritual make-up constituted a 'frail harmony' for Renan, in which the fragile beauty of Hellenism though favoured – as evinced by the rhapsodic account of his 1865 visit to Athens which appears in his *Recollections of My Youth* – could not be sustained.

Renan's primary purpose in his biography of Jesus was – in a phrase that invited a storm of protest at his inaugural lecture at the Collège de France in February 1863 – to vindicate his naturalistic view of 'this incomparable man'. There can be no doubt that he was fully conscious of the role he was playing in detaching the second person of the trinity from what George Steiner called the 'hybrid of monotheistic ideals and polytheistic practices' that constituted the faith of the Christian churches (Steiner 1971, 37). Students and scholars of Renan's writings have long been aware of this, as they have of his preference for the 'Aryan' culture of Europe over the 'Semitic' religion of the Near East. What lends a contour to his 1861 journey to the Holy Land that is anything but arcane or picturesque is his situation of these elements within a Near Eastern topography and the inclusion of a further dimension which amounts to nothing less than a *Kulturkampf* against all things Islamic. We could say that Renan's visit enabled him to place his finger upon the pulse of European and Near Eastern futures from his day to our own. Beginning with the deconstruction of western civilisation's pivotal belief in Christianity, he traces a trajectory that would lead to a re-paganised Europe declaring war upon itself, in the process massacring, incinerating and expelling its Jewish population. Renan's hatred of the Semitic principle might be seen as part of a vain effort to escape what Steiner called 'the single, unimaginable, rigorously-speaking "unthinkable", God of the Decalogue' (Steiner 1971, 38).

After Henriette had been buried in Lebanon, Renan went home to promote a message in which his sister – the first in the family to disbelieve in traditional Christianity and his most faithful supporter – had fervently believed. In 1863 he both published his *Life of Jesus* and delivered his inflammatory inaugural lecture in which he not only proclaimed the divine Son of God to be a man, but also laid out his view of the inevitable struggle of European culture against the Semitic principle, once embodied in Judaism, now resurrected in an Islam that was a bar to modern civilisation and progress:

the eternal war, the war that will not cease until the last son of Ishmael dies of poverty or has been relegated to the depths of the desert. Islam is the complete negation of Europe; Islam is fanaticism...; Islam is disdain for science, the suppression of civil society; it is the dreadful simplicity of the Semitic spirit, contracting the human brain, closing it to every delicate idea, every fine sentiment, to all rational research, to place it opposite an eternal tautology: God is God. (Renan 1947–61, 332–3)

He may have been right in declaring 'Syria is not a nationality, but ... one of the capital individualities of humanity. Strangers will organise it politically, but it will always be a region sui generis.' (Renan 1904, 162) In due course his contempt for the Muslims and Greek Orthodox Christians of Lebanon and championing of the Maronites would find confirmation of sorts in the French-inspired creation of a Lebanese state separated from the rest of Syria. The buried hatchet of hatred would be resurrected in the struggles of 'Phoenician' Maronite against Arab Muslim, post-Christian Europe pitted against the Islamic world. Among his prescriptions is the (innocent or provocative?) suggestion that 'the Mosque of Omar be replaced by a square edifice, built in that style which permits a good general view of the interior, and everything will be unchanged' (Renan 1904, 173).

There we might leave Renan's year in Syria, but that perhaps would be to cast too dark a pall over it. In spiritual terms, the *Life of Jesus* leaves open a space – an ambiguous one, it must be admitted – in which the demythologised, naturalistic portrait of its subject still allows, or leans towards a future revelation, if not a resurrection. Though his Aryan Jesus represented 'the rupture with the Jewish spirit', 'the great originality of the founder' remained. Could, he asked himself, 'great originality be born again, or will the world content itself henceforth by following the ways opened by the bold creators of the ancient ages? We know not.' (Renan 1935, 225, 227) That agnostic note was all he could manage, but still he could not bring himself to deliver final sentence on his search for the unknown God.

BIBLIOGRAPHY

Bliss, F. J. (1906) *The Development of Palestine Exploration.* London, Hodder and Stoughton.
Kaufman, A. (2004) *Reviving Phoenicia: The Search for Identity in Lebanon.* London, I. B. Tauris.
Lee, D. J. (1996) *Ernest Renan: In the Shadow of Faith.* London, Duckworth.
Mott, L. F. (1921) *Ernest Renan.* New York, D. Appleton & Co.
Moxnes, H. (2003) Renan's *Vie de Jésus* as Representation of the Orient. In H. Lapin and

D. B. Martin (eds) *Jews, Antiquity, and the Nineteenth-Century Imagination*, 85–108. Bethesda, MD, University Press of Maryland.

Neville, A. (2002) Ernest Renan and the rediscovery of the Phoenicians. In J. Conroy (ed.) *Cross Cultural Travel: Papers from the Royal Irish Academy Symposium on Literature and Travel, National University of Ireland, Galway, November 2002*, 229–38. New York, Peter Lang.

Renan, E. (1862) 'The Share of the Semitic People in the History of Civilisation'. Opening lecture as chair of Hebrew at the Collège de France, 21 February 1862. *Œuvres complètes* II.

Renan, E. (1896) *Ma Sœur Henriette. Œuvres complètes* IX. English version trs. Lady Mary Lloyd *Brother and Sister, A Memorial and the Letters of Ernest and Henriette Renan*. London, William Heinemann.

Renan, E. (1904) trs. L. O'Rourke *Letters From The Holy Land: The Correspondence of Ernest Renan with M. Berthelot while gathering material in Italy and the Orient for 'The Life of Jesus.'* New York, Doubleday, Page & Company.

Renan, E. (1935) *The Life of Jesus*. London, Watts & Co.

Renan, E. (1947–61) *Correspondance, Œuvres complètes* X. Paris, Calmann.

Salibi, K. S. (1988) *A House of Many Mansions: The History of Lebanon Reconsidered*. London, I. B. Tauris.

Schweitzer, A. (1954) *The Quest for the Historical Jesus*. London, Hodder & Stoughton.

Steiner, G. (1971) *In Bluebeard's Castle*. London, Faber.

Vermes, G. (1974) *Jesus the Jew: A Historian's Reading of the Gospels*. London, Collins.

Wardman, H. W. (1964) *Ernest Renan: A Critical Biography*. London, Athlone Press.

Wilson, A. N. (1993) *Jesus*. London, Flamingo.

Theodore Ralli's Diary on his Travel to Athos (1885)

Maria-Mirka Palioura

One night in the first week of August in the year 1885 a small ship full of pilgrims reached the little harbour of Karyes, the so-called capital of Mount Athos. Among them stood a man of dreamy look and fragile presence, a painter of Greek origin, who was born in Constantinople but later moved to Paris. Theodore Ralli (1852–1909) was an orientalist, genre painter and an indefatigable traveller, who would spend several months each year from 1890 to 1904 in Cairo, where he kept an apartment and an atelier. He was also involved in the Cairo *Salon* as one of the its founding members (1891). In 1885 he decided to visit Athos with the intention of studying its Byzantine art treasures and monastic everyday life (Palioura 2008) (Fig. 1). Behind this decision lay the belief that in the monasteries of the Holy Mountain 'the most pure tradition of Byzantine art was preserved' (Neyrat 1884, 3), a conviction enjoying wide popularity at the time. As early as 1847, Dominique Papety (1847, 769–89) speaks of the many artists who wished to join him as he was preparing to leave Athens on the *Argus* and sail out to Mount Athos. They were deterred, however, upon hearing descriptions of the hardships they would have to endure during the voyage.

It should be noted that, despite the

Figure 1. L. Welden Hawkins, Ralli's portrait. Pencil and charcoal, 1887. Private collection, Greece.

increasing scientific interest in Byzantine art towards the end of the nineteenth century, the actual research on Byzantine monuments was still in its early, formative stages. They were not usually viewed as monuments in their own right and, even if they were, they were considered inferior to their classical counterparts.

Ralli entered an unfamiliar world, where time was perceived differently, an experience that lasted until the steamship took him 'back to the world' (Ralli 2004, 41). This same feeling of transcendence can be detected in the writings of foreign travellers to the east (e.g. De Vogüé 1887), and visitors to Mount Athos (Chalot 1898, 19–32).

The journey to the Holy Mountain was to have a long-lasting effect on Ralli's work, as it became an unfailing source of artistic insight. Ralli sought his inspiration

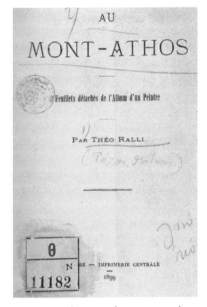

Figure 2. Title page of Au Mont-Athos, Feuillets détachés de l'Album d'un Peintre *(Ralli 1898).*

in two distinct sources: in the monastic everyday life and in the art of frescoes. It would appear that both affected his work profoundly, since in the years to come his participation in the Paris *Salon* was to take a distinctive turn. He gradually abandoned orientalistic themes in favour of Greek ones and, most importantly, of themes pertaining to the Greek Orthodox worship. His quest for new 'exotic' subjects, closer to the taste and fancies of the public and of western European art markets, led him to modern Greece with its obscure Byzantine art and its bizarre Orthodox cult practices. Ralli's relationship with this tradition and with the Greek Orthodox faith, as it emerges from his writings, is characterised by a distinctly ethnological approach and, at the same time, by a sense of respect.

Ralli was keeping a travelogue in French, extracts of which were published some years later (1899) in Cairo (Fig. 2). They first appeared as a series of short pieces in the newspaper *Chronique* and, in that same year, according to a clipping of *Journal du Caire* dated 21 January 1899 found in Ralli's *Archive* (now in the possession of the Iliaskos family), they were collected under the title *Au Mont-Athos, Feuillets détachés de l'Album d'un Peintre* (Ralli 1899). A copy of this small, rare book, originally part of the Maurocordato-Baltatzi's library, bears a handwritten dedication by the author (Ralli 2004, 13, fn. 8). It was purchased by the National Library of Greece in 1930.

The book, an octavo of 74 pages, is in very good condition. As indicated by the handwritten entry in the 'Book of Purchases' – now in the National Library's *Old Archive* – it was catalogued on 8 June 1934 and was assigned inventory number 142. Unfortunately, it has not been possible to locate Ralli's original diary or the authentic sketches and studies from his journey to Athos; only two studies and a small number of related drawings published in Greek newspapers of the period have been so far identified.

The text belongs to the type of nineteenth-century travel literature which became increasingly popular at a time when journeys into the southern region of the Balkans became more and more frequent. The purpose of the artist's visit is clearly highlighted in the diary, and his two-week tour of Athos, in August 1885, is aptly described. 'There are twenty monasteries in Mount Athos and I have but fifteen days at my disposal to see them all. In two weeks time the little steamboat will stop again at the foot of the Holy Mountain and take me back to the world.' (Ralli 2004, 41)

Our research in the Visitor's Books of the monasteries Ralli visited was strewn with difficulties and, unfortunately, did not return any results. No handwritten note attributed to the period of the painter's sojourn in Athos has been traced. The year of his visit is firmly established by the date 1885 attached on the painting *Τράπεζα σε ένα ελληνικό μοναστήρι* [*Refectory in a Greek Monastery*], for which this sojourn had been the source of inspiration. The month of his visit can be deduced by a comment made by the painter in passing with regard to the prohibition of meat during the fast observed before the feast of the Dormition of the Virgin (15 August): 'Impossible! Meat is forbidden in Athos during the first fortnight of August.' (Ralli 2004, 110)

The book is not divided into separate chapters and does not include any illustrations. In terms of language, it is characterised by a particular literary style in which understatement and poetic mood, elegance of description, directness and humour are prevalent. It is obvious from the start that the author has a taste for the picturesque and the mysterious. His narrative becomes rather detailed when it comes to describing places and landscapes. When, on the other hand, he is confronted with people, he reveals himself as a rather apt storyteller, endowed with sharp psychographic abilities. His main focus is, of course, images. The artist's travel sketches and studies are minutely documented but not at the expense of readability, since the diary makes fascinating reading throughout. A careful study of the text reveals that Ralli's later work is directly associated with his experiences in Athos. Occasionally, some rather lively and precise descriptions of his drawings and future painting projects are interjected in the text. Such descriptions, later converted into fully fledged paintings, were to take their final form in the artist's studio. On account of its importance, the diary has been translated by the author of this paper and published in Greek with an introduction, commentary and relevant illustration (Ralli 2004) (Fig. 3).

During his journey Ralli was equipped with a photographic camera along with the necessary glass plates, and carried a painting-set complete with portable easel and tubes of paint (Ralli 2004, 39). Upon arrival he had to pass through the usual entry controls, after which he spent the night in the dormitories of the little harbour. The following morning he rode to Karyes on the back of a mule. There, he was promptly received by the Holy Council (*Iera Epistasia*) before which he presented letters of recommendation (Ralli 2004, 60) obtained from the Archbishop of Athens, Procopios I. No copy or other related document was found in the Archbishop's Archive (Αρχείο Ιεράς Συνόδου, Αρχιεπισκοπή Αθηνών Ι.4, Αρχεία Φ. Αρχιεπίσκοποι, Μητροπολίται Αθηνών, Υποφ. Νο 4Γ (6), Μητροπολίτης Προκόπιος 1874–1889, Υποφ. Νο. 4Β, Μητροπολίτης Προκόπιος 1874–1889) [Prokopios I Archive]. He was subsequently granted permission to travel and stay overnight in the monasteries. The permission was accompanied by an exhortation urging the monastic community to assist him in his studies (Ralli 2004, 54). The warm welcome he received from the monks as a distinguished guest, and their unassuming hospitality, are vividly described in his diaries.

His itinerary included several stops and in his relatively short sojourn he visited no fewer than 11 of the Holy Mountain's numerous monasteries: Vatopediou, Esfigmenou, Zographou, Dohiariou, Saint Panteleimon (Russian), Simonos Petra, Grigoriou, Saint Paul's, Megisti Laura, Iviron and Koutloumousiou. Ralli travelled by foot, by boat or on the back of a mule, always in the company of a guide.

His eagerness to start drawing the minute he set foot on the Holy Mountain makes it safe to assume that he prepared numerous sketches and drawings in the course of his sojourn. A monk carrying his little luggage into a small boat, with the light of a lamp falling on him, created a rather picturesque scene which he could not resist: 'What a painting, I murmured in a mesmerised tone, quickly, a sketch.' (Ralli 2004, 38)

Although not explicitly described in the diary, his drawing of a monk painting a fresco while standing on an improvised hanging scaffold (Fig. 4) appeared in the newspaper *Journal du Caire* in 1899, probably on the occasion of the diary's publication, as attested by a clipping of *Journal du Caire* dated 21 February 1900 in Ralli's *Archive*. It depicts an interesting view of the fresco decoration of the churches or monastic buildings. Ralli's drawing dexterity together with his sharp psychographic rendering is ubiquitous in his drawings.

The artist, indefatigable in the face of hardships, unrelenting in his quest for fresh subjects, always inquisitive and curious about human nature and life, had in him the virtues of an experienced traveller and made ample use of his artistic talent in his effort to collect material that would inspire him to create works. His experiences in Athos paid off and the result of his efforts can be attested in at least three of his paintings. Working on the sketches and studies from the

Figure 3. Cover, Greek edition of Au Mont-Athos
(Ralli 2004).

Holy Mountain, he produced two works
exhibited in the Paris *Salon* of 1886. The
first in the series was *The Hagiographer:*   *Figure 4.* The Monk Iconographer, *drawing,*
A Painter of Holy Icons in Mount Athos   *signed l. r., present location unknown.*
(*Catalogue de l'Exposition de la Société des*
Artistes Français 1886, no. 1979) (Fig. 5); the painting was also shown in the 1889
Exposition Universelle (*Ράλλης (Θεόδωρος)*, in Greek, n.d. Theodore Ralli's Archive):
'Every visitor in the exhibition stands before the painting by Mr Rallis. They
admire both the unusual choice of subject and the aptitude of execution.'

Ralli had conceived the idea (Ralli 2004, 111) when he visited the monk and
icon painter Veniamin, a renowned hagiographer who lived in a monastic cell
in Karyes and who can be tentatively identified with the monk Veniamin
Kontrakis, a 'painter' and 'photographer' attested in book subscription catalogues
from Karyes up to the year 1887 (Iliou 1999, 49; Papaggelos 1998, 265, 267, fn.
85). As Ralli notes in his diary: 'I inform him that I will make a sketch of his
studio which will be my subject for the next *Salon*' (Ralli 2004, 111), and he
continues: '[T]he easel roughly-made, heavy, in a primitive style, blackened by
time ... I am in a hurry to take advantage of the beautiful light pouring through
the large opening in the roof and so I set myself before my box.' (Ralli 2004,
111–12) The scene from his diary notes is rendered with a slight variation
regarding the persons involved:

Figure 5. The Hagiographer: painter of holy icons on Mount Athos, *oil on canvas, 125 × 165 cm., 1887, J. Perdios Collection, Greece.*

Curiosity awakes me. I would very much like to see him at work. So he gets about a dozen sea shells and oysters of various colours out of a drawer. It is his palette, an egg-cup containing an egg, a plate of water in which a brush is soaking, a marble slab and a pestle and mortar to grind the colours. He places everything on the floor, near a rug in front of the easel, takes his slippers off and sits cross-legged in the Turkish fashion; and there he is, beginning to paint with his nose either close to his painting or close to his copy. (Ralli 2004, 50–51)

The second painting, *Refectory in a Greek monastery* (Fig. 6), for which the artist had a particular appreciation (Argyropoulos 1895), was also exhibited in the *Salon* of 1886 (*Catalogue de l'Exposition de la Société des Artistes Français* 1886, no. 1957). Undoubtedly, the source of his inspiration was his first impression in the monastery of Esfigmenou, as attested by the relevant excerpt:

They led me straight into the Refectory; a long room as far as the eye can see, full of monks sitting in front of long narrow tables. There were monks of all ages, all muddled up, blond, dark, tawny, white, ugly and handsome. They were eating quickly and greedily, bent over their plates. There were some who were even licking the plates, first dipping their bread in, and then plunging in their forks. Nobody was talking. We are supposed to be listening to a holy reading by a deacon, a tall good-looking boy with long blond hair who was reading in a sing-song voice from an old manuscript whose pages had a beautiful old ivory tone ... sitting alone in

Figure 6. Refectory in a Greek monastery, *1885, oil on canvas, signed l. r., present location unknown.*

Figure 7. A vision, *signed l. l., present location unknown.*

front of a small marble table is the abbot, an old man with white hands ... I had all the time to observe this place while my letters of recommendation were being handed to the abbot. (Ralli 2004, 74–7)

In addition, Ralli produced *A vision* (Fig. 7), a subject derived from the story of a young deacon whom the artist met in the monastery of Esfigmenou. The work treats the theme of temptation, taking its cue from the young man:

> His powers slowly wane, his imagination is excited, and although he struggles against the thoughts of voluptuous matters, he is possessed by the obsession of an ever present vision which awakes his feelings, dormant till now. Even when he is praying, the vision arises between him and the holy icons. (Ralli 2004, 78)

Particular features of the painting, such as the beautiful marble throne, caught his attention and the beautiful perspective of a corridor had impressed him so much that he sketched it on the spot: 'My sketch began to take shape when the abbot asked me to dine with him.' (Ralli 2004, 67) The artist made use of these sketches later when working with similar paintings. It seems that the theme of temptation appealed a lot to Ralli, since the same subject appeared in other paintings on display in the Paris *Salon* (Palioura 2008, 177).

In the works inspired by Mount Athos, the synthesis of space is faithfully rendered so as to embrace the main theme of the painting in a plausible way. An eerie atmosphere of mystery becomes the underpinning element. The theme is consistently focused on the daily routine of monastic life. In the fabric of space, Ralli adopts certain architectural elements from church interiors, a strategy which imbues his work with a new 'exotic' and picturesque texture, perceived as such by the public of the *Salon*. Through his paintings, modern Greece is firmly placed in the Orient, and his effort to collect ethnographic material becomes evident. 'Ralli, one of the best pupils of Gérôme, spent last summer several months in Greece from which he brought many and bizarre studies. The Monks of Mount Athos in the Refectory give us valuable information for the monastic costumes of the Orient.' (Clipping from *L'art et le monde*, dated 27 June 1886 in Ralli's *Archive*)

In this respect, Ralli's interest in Byzantine art does not correspond to that of other Greek artists (Papastamos 1977), who included icons in their repertoire. Ralli did not try his hand at religious painting, although he often worked on drawings and studies of church interiors in an effort to create an authentic backdrop for his subjects. Ralli's visit and apprenticeship in Athos as an icon painter is mentioned in brief amongst that of others, it is also added that 'their apprenticeship there was seen as an additional title and a quality guarantee, not only in Greece but in the Greek expatriate communities as well' (Georgiadou-Kountoura 1984, 27).

The artist's remarks go a long way in revealing his views on Byzantine art. The description of the icons found in Veniamin's workshop makes it obvious that Ralli was not yet familiar with the technique of Byzantine hagiography. He considers the hagiographers of Mount Athos at that time as: 'nothing but copyist

... they know neither how to sketch from nature nor compose. Their ambition is to slavishly imitate some figures which Byzantine painters depicted in their churches.' (Ralli 2004, 51)

He is conscious of a decline in the post-Byzantine pictorial arts, a fact which had not escaped the attention of other visitors to Mount Athos. However, he believes that there were some notable examples of frescos preserved in their original state, whereas later 'the design flags, details are neglected, the colour becomes blatant', and yet they 'show, in their simplicity, a religious feeling that is not without merit' (Ralli 2004, 51).

Ralli is not fond of the new trend in monastic art, which was heavily influenced by western motifs and nineteenth-century lithographed icons of Russian origin. For Ralli the new way of rendering the human figure completely missed the point, since this kind of art failed to inspire piety and spirituality. His artistic instinct, in spite of his ignorance of the old Byzantine art, made him appreciate the artistic value of older frescoes in the monasteries of Athos. His adamant refusal to retouch the frescoes in the refectory of the monastery of Megisti Lavra, where he was asked to 'liven up' the colours, bears witness to that effect (Ralli 2004, 105).

Interestingly enough, Islam is alluded to twice in his travelogue, and rather prominently at that, since both references correspond to the pivotal moments of the beginning and the end of his stay at Athos (Neyrat 1884, 3). The published text begins and ends with the Shahadah recited by Muslim fellow passengers in the vessel that carries Ralli to and from the Holy Mountain. It should be borne in mind that at the time Mount Athos was still under Ottoman sovereignty. *Shahadah* is the Islamic creed. Although it is not actually included in the Quran it amounts to a concise declaration of Islam's central tenet: *lâ ilâha illallâh, Muḥammadun rasûlullâh* 'There is no God but Allah, and Muhammad is the Messenger of Allah.' (*Encyclopédie de l'Islam 1936*, s.v. 'Shahadah')

This intriguing juxtaposition of the Muslim and Christian element may be attributed to his undisputed cosmopolitanism and his origins in Constantinople, which contributed to the development of tolerance towards the 'other'.

The association between the works he created and the places he visited becomes evident in the text of his diary – the paintings presented in this paper bear witness to that effect. This straightforward combination of sketches and written word results in the closest imaginable correlation between the two media.

Ralli's diary is an important source of information for the study of modern Greek art. It offers valuable insights on Athos and is probably the earliest description of the Holy Mountain handed down to us by a Greek artist.

BIBLIOGRAPHY

Argyropoulos, M. (1895) 'Ο ζωγράφος Ράλλης', *Αμάλθεια*, 16–28 November.

Catalogue de l'Exposition de la Société des Artistes Français (1886). No. 1957 Réfectoire dans un couvent grec – 1885; No. 1979 L'iconographe; peintre des saintes images au Mont Athos, catalogue illustré, 254.

Chalot, Le Comte de (1898) Dans un pays de moines, *Revue des revues et Revue d'Europe et d'Amérique*, 1ère année, IIIe série, XXV, 7, 1 April.

De Vogüé, E. M. (1887) *Syrie, Palestine, Mont Athos, voyage aux pays du passé*, 3rd edn, Paris.

Houtsma, M. T. *et al.*, eds (1913–38) *Encyclopédie de l'Islam: Dictionnaire géographique, ethnographique et biographique des peuples musulmans* (1913–38). Publié avec le concours des Principaux orientalistes. 4 vols. avec Suppl. Leyden, Brill and Paris, Picard.

Georgiadou-Kountoura, E. (1984) *Θρησκευτικά θέματα στη Νεοελληνική ζωγραφική 1900–1940*, Thessaloniki.

Iliou, F. (1999) 'Αγιογράφοι, ζωγράφοι, χαράκτες και σταμπαδόροι, Η μαρτυρία των καταλόγων συνδρομητών', *Μεταβυζαντινά χαρακτικά, Πρακτικά επιστημονικής ημερίδας*, Μουσείο Βυζαντινού Πολιτισμού, 10 November 1995, Greek Ministry of Culture.

Neyrat, L'Abbé A. S. (1884) *L' Athos: Notes d'une excursion à la presqu'île et la montagne des moines*.

Palioura, M. (2008) *The work of Theodore Ralli (1852-1909): Sources of inspiration – Orientalistic subjects* (PhD Thesis, Athens University, Department of Archaeology and History of Art [*Το ζωγραφικό έργο του Θεόδωρου Ράλλη (1852-1909): Πηγές έμπνευσης - Οριενταλιστικά θέματα*, διδακτ. διατριβή, Εθνικό Καποδιστριακό Πανεπιστήμιο Αθηνών, Τμήμα Ιστορίας- Αρχαιολογίας]

Papaggelos, I. (1998) Περί των Γαλατσιάνων ζωγράφων του Αγίου Όρους Από τη Μεταβυζαντινή Τέχνη στη Σύγχρονη 18ος -20ός αι., *Πρακτικά Πανελλήνιου Συνεδρίου, Α. Π.Θ.* Thessaloniki, Aristotelian University of Thessaloniki, University Studio Press.

Papastamos, D. (1977), *Η επίδραση της Ναζαρηνής σκέψης στη Νεοελληνική εκκλησιαστική ζωγραφική*. Athens.

Papety, D. (1847) Les peintures byzantines et les couvents de l' Athos *Revue des Deux Mondes* XVIII.

Ralli, T. (1899) *Au Mont Athos, Feuillets détachés de l'Album d'un Peintre par Théo Ralli*. Cairo, Imprimerie Centrale.

Ralli, T. (2004) *Στο Όρος Άθως, Αποσπάσματα από το ημερολόγιο ενός ζωγράφου, Υπό Θεόδωρου Ράλλη* (εισαγωγή-μτφ.-σχόλια Μ. Παλιούρα). [*At Mount Athos, Extracts from a Painter's diary by Theodore Ralli* (translation, introduction, commentary M. Palioura]. Athens, Editions Kastaniotis.

Men in Skirts and How to Become Frank

John Chapman

In November 1809, Byron, then in Epirus, added a postscript to his letter to his mother. 'I have some very "magnifique" Albanian dresses the only expensive articles in this country they cost 50 guineas each & have so much gold they would cost in England two hundred.' (Marchand 1973, 231)

Probably not the first but undoubtedly the most famous foreigner to dress up in a fustanella, Byron only wore the costume once in England and that was to sit, or rather stand, for the famous portrait by Thomas Phillips. There are over 30 variations of this portrait – some waist upwards, some full length – though all are discreetly vague about Byron's clubfoot. Another cosmetic addition, and it is not clear at whose suggestion, was a moustache for Byron. It was thought that bare-lipped he would look too effeminate in the Albanian garb.

This portrait confirmed the romantic view of Greece to a public over-eager to conflate Byron with Childe Harold and the Corsair. And that was probably the result that the poet and his publisher, John Murray, intended. Strangely, Byron gave away the costume to a friend to wear at a ball. In his letter to Miss Mercer Elphinstone in early May 1814 Byron wrote:

> I send you the Arnaout garments – which will make an admirable costume for a Dutch Dragoon. – The Camesa or *Kilt* (to speak Scottishly) you will find very long – it is the custom with the Beys and sign of rank to wear it to the ancle – I know not why – but so it is – the million shorten it to the knee which is more antique – and becoming – at least those who have legs and a propensity to show them ... if you like the dress – keep it – I shall be very glad to get rid of it – as it reminds me of one or two things I don't wish to remember. (Marchand 1975, 113)

One could spend many prurient hours speculating on what Byron is alluding to, but the fact of the matter is that the fustanella and its associated garments impressed the western onlooker. As late as the 1850s, the American writer Jane Anthony Eames positively gushed when she visited Greece:

I am perfectly in love with the costume worn by the men; the full kirtle, the richly embroidered gaiters and jackets, the large open sleeve flowing behind and displaying the full sleeve of the shirt, dazzlingly clean and white, the red cap, hanging gracefully down one side, with its long blue tassel, combined with the graceful walk of these men, make them look like heroes on a stage. (Eames 1855, 133–4)

Figure 1. Byron in Albanian costume. George Gordon Byron, 6th Baron Byron by William Finden; after Thomas Phillips. © National Portrait Gallery, London.

But the fustanella was not the national costume of Greece. Nearly all foreign commentators correctly identified it as 'Albanian' and certainly many Greeks, on the mainland and the islands, wore pantaloons and other garbs. The adoption of the fustanella by the Greeks can be seen as a male fashion statement with political overtones, especially as it was adopted by pre-revolutionary Klephts or bandits who then became heroes of the Greek War of Independence – Kolokotronis, Makriyiannis *et al.* – and this image was assiduously portrayed in the pictorial romanticising of the struggle for Greek freedom.

We can observe that, at the same time as the fustanella was being adopted by the Greeks as their national costume, the western European male was adopting the look of Beau Brummell, the monochrome dandy, which confined male dress to the black suit and the starched white shirt for the remainder of the nineteenth and much of the following centuries.

In western male society colour was eschewed, in fact it has been referred to as 'the great renunciation' (Harvey 1995) and the only chance to 'dress up' was in uniform or for the Masquerade, a popular escape. In an attack on Sir William Gell's 'Narrative of a Journey in the Morea' in 1823 the *Edinburgh Review* wrote:

Bound as we are to warn 'the reading public' against all hawkers of spurious commodities, we really cannot recommend this work to their notice; but we think it fair to add, that it may be of considerable use to the owners of Masquerade warehouses, as containing some choice descriptions of breeches, sashes and waistcoats, which we have no doubt, might prove serviceable in making up an Oriental costume. (*Edinburgh Review* 1823, 332)

The *Edinburgh Review*'s vituperation was aimed at Gell's contention that the Greek revolution was doomed to failure due to intrinsic weaknesses of the Greek character. But many others had another view, which led them to travel to Greece and volunteer to fight. They started out in their western costumes. Contemporary prints show the Philhellenes of 1822 in their ragged western uniforms; they soon found out that Greece was a very hard and stony place and clothes quickly fell apart. It was also an advantage to discard their western rags; you merged in, you were no longer an obvious Frangoi – Frank, the catch-all name Greeks gave to western foreigners. It was also practical, there being no western tailors. There are portraits of many important Philhellenes; the Frenchman Fabvier, the American Samuel Gridley Howe and an Englishman Edgar Garston, all in Greek costume.

Garston spent a number of years in Greece fighting side by side with Greeks. He later reminisced of an occasion in Hydra when, noting a British naval officer having linguistic difficulties,

> I went down to the water-side to offer my assistance as interpreter. He and his boat's crew were not a little astonished when I addressed him in English, for I was accoutred as a Pallekar, and, having recently come over from the Morea, my petticoat was not of dazzling whiteness. (Garston 1842, 21)

Garston also points to the reality of living in one's costume in wartime, when he meets up with his ex-comrades some 15 years later:

> One of these, Capt. Salafattini, is now a grim old warrior of sixty, with beard as black, teeth as white, and step as firm, as when I scrambled over the mountains with him in 1825. He is still the true Mainote pallekar, and knows only his God, his country, and his chief. Among other circumstances of a less trifling nature which he recalled, my efforts to keep my dress cleaner and more free from *inhabitants* than that of my comrades, were not forgotten. (Garston 1842, 241)

Garston was obviously proud of his ability to disappear into the oriental scene. In another anecdote he recalled being asked by the captain of HMS Seringapatam to negotiate with local Greeks. Garston decided it was sensible to dress up in his fustanella and turban, and was idly chatting with an officer when the Captain appeared on deck. 'As soon as his eye fell upon me, he stopped short, and addressing the officer of the watch, "How is it," said he, "that you allow *these people* to come on board without reporting it to me?" He had taken me for one of the natives, and the error (?) caused no little amusement.' (Garston 1842, 33).

It may seem odd that Byron, of all the Philhellenes, did not adopt the Albanian dress when in Greece. Admittedly he did invent himself a rather ludicrous faux ancient plumed helmet, but he generally kept to Frankish dress, along with the Greek leader whom he most respected, the western educated and dressed Alexander Mavrocordatos.

With the liberation of Greece there came a moment of decision for the Greeks. Which way would the new nation align itself, to the orient or to the western powers who had brokered the winning of the war? The first president of the land was Iaonnis Kapodistrias, a Corfiot long in Russian diplomatic circles. Kapodistrias was the polar opposite to the Pallikars in their wild dresses. Cold, precise and controlling, Kapodistrias wore the Frankish male black civilian dress code. When he locked away the leader of the vengeful Maniates, Petrobey Mavromichalis, in Napflion in October 1831, he was approached by Petrobey's son Giorgos and brother Konstantinos to plead for their leader's release. They had, to impress, dressed up to the nines in their Albanian finery. Kapodistrias rejected their demands but could not help but pass comment on the extravagance of their costumes when Greece was in deep crisis. 'Today the President put me to shame,' said Georgios (Woodhouse 1973, 390). On the morning of Sunday 9th October 1831 Giorgos and Konstantinos assassinated Kapodistrias.

Admittedly their motives were by no means solely a matter of being ticked off for their flashy dress, but one can ascertain a tension between different conventions of costume amongst the inhabitants of the nascent Greek state. One of the Mavromichalis clan complained that everything had become 'Frank'. The confusion was compounded when France, Britain and Russia presented Greece with a king from Bavaria, Otto, later joined by his Queen Amalia from Oldenburg and accompanied by a host of Bavarian civil servants and soldiers. Otto and his delight in the Greek dress deserve more attention than this paper allows me, save to note that even after being forced to abdicate by the Greeks, he spent much of his declining years in Bavarian exile dressed in the fustanella and Albanian waistcoat.

A sketch, by the Bavarian Ludwig Köllnberger, of an 1830s coffee house in Athens epitomises the clear divide between those Greeks in Frankish costume and those in the fustanella, each group sitting on opposite sides of the room, and clearly despising the other. Perhaps no other modern nation has gone through such contortions of forging an identity as the Greek, and this cannot have been helped by the number of travellers who came to look, observe and then pass judgment, in a veritable deluge of books and articles.

One visitor was clearly intending to add to the volumes on Greece. In 1838 Henry Herbert, third Earl of Carnarvon, took his wife and two eldest children on a planned Grand Tour of Europe which would take in France, Italy, Greece, Turkey and eventually, he hoped, the Holy Land and Egypt. He landed at Piraeus in February 1839 armed with servants, nannies, notebooks, journal, sketchbook and a portable writing desk. He was delighted by the Greek costume, 'the beauty of which far exceeded my expectations' (Carnarvon 1839, 26 February):

> the variety of the costume charms me – the capote dark but beautifully flowered the rich figured waistcoat of various colours the sash the fustanella or white

Figure 2. The Athenian kafeneion (café). 'Beautiful Greece' 1836. Watercolour by Hans Hanke after the original by Ludwig Köllnberger. © National Historical Museum, Athens.

> petticoat and the variety of headdresses folded sometimes in light and twisted forms sometimes loosely like the turban and the hair arranged in a thousand different ways were all incidents of a minor kind that were very delightful. (Carnarvon 1839, 5 March)

Carnarvon was also delighted by the female dress and, at a state ball, positively ogled the daughter of the famous hero of the Greek War of Independence, Markos Bozzaris. She was in his words:

> a singularly beautiful young woman whose really great personal attractions were enhanced by the Greek dress which she wore. The effect of the red bonnet which she carried on her head most gracefully on one side & the long tassel which hung down was very bewitching – the upper part of her dress was tight the arms tight & cut in rather a formal shape offering the bosom naturally like the dress in Puritan days. (Carnarvon 1839. 14 March)

Carnarvon also encountered more modern Greek ladies. One of his contacts was the family of James Skene. Skene Junior, Henry, had married a Phanariot Greek, Rhalou Rizou-Rangavi:

> She has a great deal of conversation and speaks French well; we differed however terribly on one point she quite approves of the disuse of the Greek costume; the reason she gives is that in the women it leads to Turkish habits indolence difficulty

of moving about from long training but the real reason is manifestly for that she comments at last the dress being oriental and not European – Why said she should we be different from the rest of Europe we ought to become like it and this is the real secret of many of those to the political considerations that attach to the dress are still overthrowing the Greek costume. The vanity of being European in all respects prevails over national feeling and will throw over all that is distinctive & characteristic. We sparred a little on this subject but she is a very agreeable woman and has much to say (Carnarvon 1839, 13 March)

Carnarvon was, it must be admitted, a nostalgic romantic, and although he stuck to western dress during his travels in Greece he could not but help purchase costumes for his son 'Bab' and daughter Eveline, who were sketched in 1840 in their miniature Greek attire on their return to England.

Carnarvon's lament for the decline of Greek costume is the age-old tourist cry of 'Oh it isn't the same as it used to be...' He wrote in his journal:

the air of the commonest Greek in his Greek dress is peculiarly dignified they have a haughty kind of bearing which imposes; this is strong even in the peasant; in the chief extremely so – All this is lost when they dress in the European style & they look perfectly insignificant & as if ashamed of themselves – but the dress though worn by the mass is going out. (Carnarvon 1839, 9 April)

It is odd that the word fashion did not crop up. The most obvious factor in driving women's fashion, in Athens that is, was the desire to wear the latest French fashions. The American Henry M. Baird wrote in an 1856 volume of an Athenian wedding:

The assembled company, composed as usual of a much greater proportion of ladies than of gentlemen, were mostly dressed in the latest style of Paris fashions. Yet there was a sprinkling of gentlemen clad in the genuine Albanian dress, comprising your free-and-easy people who wish to pass for the more independent class of society, and scorn to adopt the perpetually changing mode. (Baird 1856, 89)

And Baird cannot resist a patronising dig:

All the tight lacing in the world could not give an Athenian young lady the wasp-like contour which is the admiration of French dressmakers and misses in their teens. Disguise it as they may, there is a tendency to embonpoint among the ladies, many of whom waddle about with a grace which would seem charming in the eyes of our Dutch progenitors. (Baird 1856, 9)

In urban locations the fustanella was on its way out but a number of observations show that there was an odd mixture of old and new. There was also a curious western appreciation of the change – mostly the Frangoi could not make up their mind whether it was a good thing or not, though their western mind-set tended to equate Frankish dress with progress. Sir Thomas Wyse, British Minister in Greece, made a tour of the Peloponnese in 1858 where at Monemvasia:

Figure 3. Alexandros Koumoundouros at Zarnata Castle, Mani, Greece, 1868.

> The authorities were already there to meet us. The Eparch, a silent, jejune man in
> island trousers; the Demarch, in creditably clean fustanella; and the doctor, in
> Frank dress, presenting a good epitome of the transition through which manners
> and costumes are hastening in Greece. (Wyse 1865, 5)

Wyse later noted in Kalamata the prevalence of native costume, especially in
the women:

> the explanation was simple and satisfactory, and made without rhetorical
> pretensions to patriotism. The costume, it was said, is uniform, economical, and
> intelligible to every Greek; it can be made – material and fashion – at home, and
> does not require "le petit follet des dames", or any extra rivalry between them
> and their neighbours. (Wyse 1865, 233)

But things were getting confused.

A photograph of Alexandros Koumoundouros, who managed to be Prime
Minister of Greece a record ten times, was taken in 1868 on a visit to the castle
of Zarnata, his home village, in Mani. Here we can observe Koumoundouros in
his frock-coat surrounded by strange admixture of his countrymen in fustanella
and Frankish dress.

And the western observer was becoming more circumspect. This '*Conversations
at Athens on Local Topics. Scene – The terrace of the house of a resident at Athens*' is a
curiosity from *Fraser's Magazine* of September 1860 (375–6):

> RESIDENT   By the way, how do you find your present quarters?
> CAPITALIST I can't say much for the Hotel d'Orient: it is very dirty, and the host,
> named Yany, is a fat slovenly sort of fellow.

RESIDENT   I am not surprised at what you say, for the hotel may have changed for the worse, like its landlord. This Yany used to wear a year or two ago the fustanella, or dress of the country; he was then smart enough, and his stomach did not show so much. He used then to speak, nay, almost to boast of having been a pirate; in the capacity of host his occupation is probably but little modified, though he has put away the dress of the Klephts.

In 1882 the classical scholar Henry Tozer and his constant travelling companion the Bursar of Corpus Christi, T. M. Crowder, visited Itilon in Mani; they too made a differentiation between those in the old costume and those in the Frankish.

In the course of the evening the physician of the town and another gentleman, M. Zanglès, presented themselves. The former of these was quite a man of the old school, for he wore the fustanella and a large belt containing pistols ... His companion was dressed in the costume of Western Europe. (Tozer 1882, 357–8)

Twenty or so years later, when members of the British School at Athens visited the backwater of Mani, there was not a fustanella to be seen and the local doctors looked much like their western contemporaries.

Charles Dudley Warner further reported in 1875, on his way from Piraeus to Athens:

At a half-way inn, where we stopped to water the horses, there was a hostler in the Albanian, or as it is called, the Grecian national costume, wearing the fustanella and the short jacket: but the stiff white petticoat was rumpled and soiled, and I fancied he was somewhat ashamed of the half-womanly attire, and shrank from inspection, like an actor in a harlequin dress, surprised by daylight outside the theatre. (Warner 1875, 339)

Slowly but surely the fustanella became the costume of the provinces or the tourist trade. When Thomas Cook's sons opened their first branch in Athens, to advertise it they naturally dressed up in fustanellas.

Oscar Wilde, along with many other Victorian infant males forced into skirts, probably swore blind he would never wear one again after his childhood frights. 'Oh, you will Oscar, you will.' When he visited Greece with his Professor John Pentland Mahaffy in April 1877 he visited a photographic studio in Athens; the result – a delightful photograph of Oscar in a fustanella.

Finally I return to Edgar Garston and that word masquerade. Garston became a prosperous Liverpool merchant of radical persuasions. Some time in his fifties or sixties he paid a photographer to take pictures of him in his Albanian outfit which he had brought back from Greece. In fact he had already posed in this outfit for the Italian artist Francesco Hayez on his way home in the 1820s. Although he adopted the fustanella during the Greek War of Independence out of practicality, he knew a theatrical costume when he saw it – and, like most of us, Garston enjoyed dressing up.

Last word with Garston. In 1840 he was in Greece during the carnival, and from his window he observed the masquerade in the street below. Most Athenians wore their native dress, but Garston spotted something much more interesting:

Figure 4. Oscar Wilde photographed in Athens. April 1877. © British Library Board. dd.81783A

Among the masks of this day, which in general were badly dressed and without meaning, I observed one group which was by no means deficient in character. It was composed of two individuals dressed as Europeans of fashion, attended by a third in the Turkish dress, carrying an umbrella, camp-stool, &c.- representing two European travellers and their dragoman. From time to time the Franks would make a halt, take out their portfolios, and be seemingly intently occupied in taking a sketch, or in drawing the portrait of some one whom they would stop for that purpose. Anon they would enter into conversation with another of the passers by, through the medium of their attendant, as if themselves ignorant of the country, and affecting to be much struck with some remark or reply, would take out their note-books and set it down therein, with an air of infinite satisfaction. It was really a good practical satire upon the bearing of many European travellers. (Garston 1842, 94)

BIBLIOGRAPHY

Baird, H. (1856) *Modern Greece: a Narrative of a Residence and Travels in that Country.* New York, Harper & Brothers.

Carnarvon, Third Earl (Herbert H.) (1839) Unpublished journal ms. Somerset Records Office, Taunton.

Eames, J. (1860) *The Budget Closed.* Boston, Ticknor and Fields.

Edinburgh Review (1823).

Fraser's Magazine for Town & Country (1860) September.

Garston, E. (1842) *Greece Revisited and Sketches in Lower Egypt, in 1840.* London, Saunders & Otley.

Harvey, J. (1995) *Men in Black.* London, Reaktion Books.

Marchand, L. (1973) *'In my hot youth'; Byron's Letters and Journals. Volume 1.* London, John Murray.

Marchand, L. (1975) *'Wedlock's the devil'; Byron's Letters and Journals. Volume 4*. London, John Murray.

Tozer, H. (1882) Vitylo and Cargese. *The Journal of Hellenic Studies* 3, 354–60.

Warner, C. (1876) *In the Levant*. Boston, Houghton Mifflin & Co.

Woodhouse, C. (1973) *Capodistria: The Founder of Greek Independence*. London, Oxford University Press.

Wyse, T. (1865) *An Excursion in the Peloponnesus in the Year 1858*. London, Day & Son Ltd.

Index

Entries in italics denote pages with illustrations